Woodworker's Tool Guide

Woodworker's
Tool Guide

*Getting the Most from Your Hand Tools,
Power Tools & Accessories*

David Day & Albert Jackson

Sterling Publishing Co., Inc.
New York

WOODWORKER'S TOOL GUIDE
Conceived, edited and designed at Inklink,
Greenwich, London, England

Text: Albert Jackson and David Day

Design and art direction: Simon Jennings

Text editors: Albert Jackson and Peter Leek

Illustrators: Robin Harris and David Day

Studio photography: Neil Waving and Ben Jennings

Indexer: Mary Morton

Proofreader: Mary Morton

For HarperCollins:

Editorial director: Polly Powell

Senior production manager: Bridget Scanlon

Library of Congress
Cataloging-in-Publication Data Available

10 9 8 7 6 5 4 3 2 1

Published in 1997 by Sterling Publishing Company, Inc.
387 Park Avenue South, New York, N.Y. 10016

Originally published in 1997 by HarperCollins*Publishers*,
London, under the title *Good Wood Tools*

Distributed in Canada by Sterling Publishing
c/o Canadian Manda Group, One Atlantic Avenue, Suite 105
Toronto, Ontario, Canada M6K 3E7

Text set in Franklin Gothic Extra Condensed, Univers Condensed
and Garamond Book Condensed by Inklink, London

Printed in Singapore

Jacket photograph: Ben Jennings

Sterling ISBN 0-8069-0511-5

CONTENTS

INTRODUCTION

You would find it hard to persuade professional carpenters or cabinet-makers to lend you their tools, and they would not be entirely happy about working with someone else's plane or handsaw. They tend to guard their tools jealously in order to preserve something that cannot be bought and which may have taken years to acquire – a custom-made tool kit. The way a person stands at the bench, the way he or she adjusts and holds their tools, even the way they sharpen them, eventually shapes and modifies those tools until they work better for their owners than for anyone else. Tools are important because they are quite literally the means to an end, and there is no shortcut to becoming proficient with them. Specialized knowledge can be helpful, sound technique is essential, but ultimately there is no substitute for practical experience. This book aims to bridge the gap between theory and practice.

ACKNOWLEDGMENTS

Reference material and equipment

The authors and producers are grateful to the following for supplying reference and equipment used in this book:

Roy Arnold, Ipswich, Suffolk
Axminster Power Tool Centre, Axminster, Devon
Black & Decker Professional Products Division, Slough, Berkshire
The Black & Decker Corporation, Slough, Berkshire
John Boddy's Fine Wood & Tool Store Ltd., Boroughbridge, Yorkshire
Robert Bosch Ltd., Uxbridge, Middlesex
Buck & Hickman Ltd., Sheffield, S. Yorkshire
Draper Tools Ltd., Eastleigh, Hampshire
Elu Power Tools Ltd., Slough, Berkshire
Emmerich (Berlon) Ltd., Ashford, Kent
Garrett Wade, New York, NY, USA
Record Marples Ltd., Sheffield, S. Yorkshire
Mark & Jane Rees
Robert Sorby Ltd., Sheffield, S. Yorkshire
The Stanley Works Ltd., Sheffield, S. Yorkshire
Alec Tiranti Ltd., Theale, Berkshire
Tilgear Ltd., Cuffley, Hertfordshire
Veritas Tools, BriMarc Associates, Warwick, Warwickshire

Photography

The studio photographs for this book were taken by Neil Waving, with the following exceptions:

Paul Chave, pages 14, 62, 63 (T), 64
Ben Jennings, pages 3, 5, 76 (T), 78, 92 (T)

The authors and producers also acknowledge additional photography by, and the use of photographs from, the following individuals and companies:

Black & Decker Professional Products Division, Slough, Berkshire, page 31
The Black & Decker Corporation, Slough, Berkshire, page 85 (B)
Robert Bosch Ltd., Uxbridge, Middlesex, pages 90 (T), 91
Draper Tools Ltd., Eastleigh, Hampshire, page 116
Georg Ott Werkzeug-Und Maschinen Fabric GMBH & Co., Germany, page 107 (R)
Record Marples Ltd., Sheffield, S. Yorkshire, page 112

Key to credits

T = top, B = bottom, L = left, R = right, TL = top left, TC = top centre, TR = top right, CL = centre left, C = centre, CR = centre right, BL = bottom left, BC = bottom centre, BR = bottom right

CHAPTER 1 A Victorian cabinetmaker might be baffled by present-day power tools, but show him a kit of modern handtools and he would be the master of them in no time. The same goes for woodworkers from almost any period in history, because many of the tools we use today are simply improved versions of those that have been employed for centuries – some have hardly changed at all.

FORERUNNERS

SAWING & CLEAVING

Our forebears used two methods to convert logs into usable lumber: they either sawed them into planks, a laborious task before the Industrial Revolution, or they split the wood along the grain.

Frame saws and open saws

The basic concept of a toothed saw for cutting wood goes back thousands of years, but it was the idea of holding a narrow blade under tension, coupled with setting teeth alternately to reduce friction, that made for efficient saws capable of accurate work. Hence the widespread use of frame saws. Some of these were similar to today's curve-cutting saws, while others were large ripsaws or crosscutting saws.

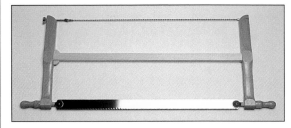

Modern frame saw

The ability to manufacture rolled-steel strip led to the possibility of an unsupported blade that would not buckle. The new generation of "open" saws with a handgrip at one end of the blade were the precursors of our present-day handsaws.

Sixteenth-century joiner's workshop
The craftsman in the foreground is cross-cutting with a saw that is almost identical to the modern frame saw (top right).

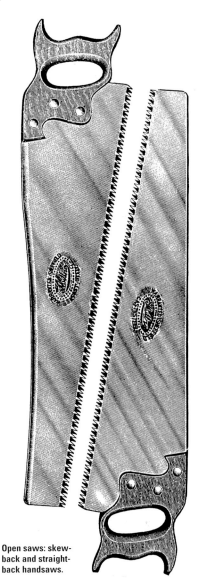

Open saws: skew-back and straight-back handsaws.

Two-man crosscut and pitsaws

One exception to the standard open-saw pattern was the hefty two-man crosscut saw which was used to fell trees, then convert them into logs for transportation. Another was the pitsaw, designed solely for ripsawing. A crosscut saw generally had two identical handles, whereas a pitsaw had a short, easily detachable crossbar or "box" at one end and a tiller for steering the saw at the other.

Once the standard method for converting lumber, pitsawing was hard labor, especially for the "box man," who spent his working day beneath the log, covered in sweat and sawdust. The senior sawyer, who worked on top, was responsible for marking out the log and steering the saw on its intended path.

The log was supported on trestles or suspended above a pit. Plank widths were sawn one by one down to the first support, at which stage the saw was dismantled and the log repositioned so that the work could continue. To prevent the partly sawn planks from vibrating, wedges were driven into the kerfs behind the saw and the end of the log tightly bound with rope.

Froes

For some trades it was more profitable to split wood lengthwise, rather than expend the energy required to saw it by hand. The log itself was cleaved into radial sections, using wedges and a maul – an ax-like tool with a thick, wedge-shaped head. Splitting these sections into shingles or into straight-grain billets for turning or shaving was accomplished with a froe. The froe has a thick blade that is driven into the end grain with a heavy wooden mallet or club until a split develops; levering on the froe's handle twists the blade and extends the split. Froes and mauls are still offered for sale.

Using a froe to split wood is a traditional alternative to sawing.

MEASURING & MARKING

The first ever system of "standard" measurement was based on parts of the human body: the fathom (the distance spanned by a man's outstretched arms); the cubit (elbow to tip of middle finger); the span (the distance between the tips of the thumb and little finger of an outstretched hand); the palm (the width of four fingers); and the digit (the width of one finger). The Romans introduced the foot and also the inch (uncia), which corresponds to the width of the thumb. These dimensions were gradually refined into various statutory systems of measurement, culminating in the current imperial system. The metric system was devised in eighteenth-century France to replace a chaotic amalgam of different standards.

Rules and tape measures

The earliest carpenter's rules were strips of wood, inscribed and stamped by hand. Folding rules date from around 1600. The forerunners of printed fabric tapes and steel tape measures were, simply, knotted cords.

Squares and marking gauges

At one time squares were made entirely from wood, but by the middle of the eighteenth century woodworkers were making their own squares and bevels with metal blades. Right up until the second half of the nineteenth century, marking gauges were simple tools, typically made from beech, with a sliding stock held in place by a captive wedge or a wooden thumbscrew. Contemporary mortise gauges were fitted with pairs of fixed pins, so a carpenter had to have a variety of gauges to meet his needs.

HEWING & SHAVING

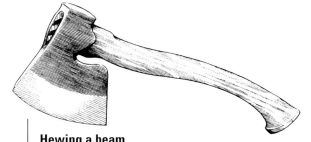

From ancient times, axes and adzes have been used to square and dress lumber; smaller components were shaped with crudely made drawknives. The same methods were still being practiced in rural industries at the beginning of the twentieth century and even today some craftsmen keep the tradition alive.

Hewing axes and hatchets

The axe is one of the oldest of woodworking tools, developed and modified over time to suit the particular requirements of various trades. The side or broad axe is typical, being used to square and pare components as diverse as ship's lumbers, house beams and chair legs. There were full-size axes and smaller hatchets, selected according to the scale of the work. Side axes, usually in the form of hatchets, are still included in modern tool catalogs.

A side ax has a curved cutting edge that produces a slicing action; and, because the blade is usually beveled on one side only, it can be presented to the work at a shallow angle. The shaft is offset or cranked to provide knuckle clearance.

Hewing a beam

There was no prescribed method for hewing wood, since each individual woodsman or artisan would have developed his or her own preferred technique, but generally a barked log would have been supported off the ground on crossbeams and secured with simple iron staples known as "dogs" to prevent it rolling.

Using chalked cord, straight lines were snapped along each side of the log to mark the width of the beam, then the top surface was chopped crosswise down to the lines to divide the waste into sections. The log was then rolled through 90 degrees so that the crosscut surface could be hewn.

With one knee pressed against the log, the woodworker would pare down to the marked lines with short strokes of the ax, working backwards along the log. The process was repeated until the workpiece had been squared on four sides.

Hewing produces a flat, reasonably smooth surface, but for exposed woodwork a beam was sometimes subsequently dressed with an adze to remove the marks left by crosscutting with an ax.

Hewing was a practice common to many trades. Here medieval shipwrights are preparing a beam with two-handed hewing axs.

Straight and curved-edge drawknives

Adzes

The adze is another almost obsolete tool, once used to dress lumber in order to make a flat surface. Since the cutting edge is turned at right angles to the shaft, the tool is swung with a short pendulum action towards the woodworker. A general-purpose carpenter's adze was often used to remove the bulk of the waste, but there were also relatively lightweight finishing adzes for "smoothing" the surface. Curved-head adzes were used to carve out concave bowls and traditional wooden chair seats. Two-handed carpenter's adzes and hatchet-size carving adzes are still available.

Ship carpenter's adze

Drawknives

The drawknife ranks with the ax and the adze in being a tool that was adopted by a wide variety of tradesmen from earliest times. In its simplest form the drawknife is a straight or slightly curved blade, beveled along one side. The metal at each end of the blade is forged into a pointed tang, bent at right angles and fitted with a turned handle.

The basic style of knife was used by wheelwrights and coopers. Chair makers used a similar tool to shape curved back rests and arms; and it was also used to shave wood into roughly cylindrical billets ready for turning into legs and stretcher rails on a lathe. An inshave is a conventional drawknife bent into a curve for shaping hollow chair seats, while a scorp – a tightly bent inshave with both tangs fitted into a single handle – is ideal for carving and shaping deep wooden bowls.

Cutting with an adze

Stand on the work or clamp it beneath one foot, and take up a stance that allows you to swing the adze towards you, using your thigh as a stop for your forearm (this prevents the adze from swinging too far). Take relatively thin shavings when dressing lumber.

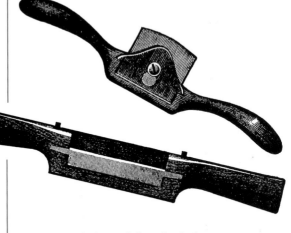

Beechwood spokeshave and all-metal spokeshave

Spokeshaves

The spokeshave has a small blade, similar to that of a drawknife, secured to the tool's wooden stock with two pointed tangs. Although it is possible to draw a spokeshave towards you, it is easier to control the tool if you hold one handle in each hand and push it away from you. The modern metal spokeshave was a development of plane making dating from the late nineteenth century.

Using a drawknife

Drawknives are designed to cut on the pull stroke, using the handles to control the depth of cut by presenting the cutting edge at just the right angle to the work. Tradesmen usually held the workpiece on a shaving horse – a purpose-made stool with a foot-operated clamp.

PLANING AND CHISELING

Smoothing or "coffin" plane

The origins of the woodworking plane are particularly obscure. Other than a few Roman tools that have come to light, there is scant evidence of what they may have looked like before the sixteenth century. At that time wooden planes are depicted with a cutter held in place with a wedge, and sporting a carved handle or horn near the toe of the tool – similar in many respects to the planes that are distributed right across Europe today. In Great Britain and America woodworkers seem to have preferred a different pattern of plane, also made from wood but with the handle set towards the heel. Wooden smoothing planes were usually made without handles.

available, and wooden planes were still in use right up until the 1940s and 1950s. If you are of a mind to do so, you can obtain identical planes today.

In addition to the full quota of wooden bench planes, the Victorian tool chest contained a selection of molding planes, rabbet planes, grooving and plow planes, all of which have been rendered obsolete by modern power routers. Even so, many of them are still available for those who want to work in the traditional manner. It is even possible to buy a basic wooden router plane that, in design, predates the metal version shown on page 63.

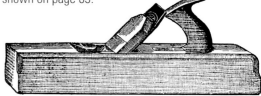

Wooden jack plane

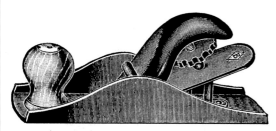

American-pattern all-metal block plane

Wood versus metal

Unlike the hewing ax and the adze, which have hardly changed since prehistoric times, the plane went through a long process of development and improvement right up until the late nineteenth century, when the fully adjustable, all-metal plane was perfected. In recent times, manufacturers have introduced a bench plane with disposable blades. However, older models tend to remain popular with traditionalists even when newer ones become

Wooden molding planes

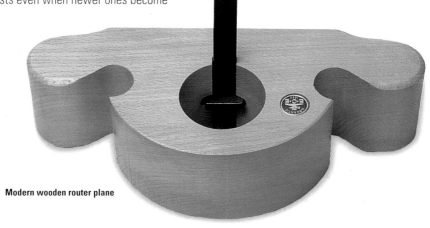

Modern wooden router plane

The joiner in the middle distance is cutting a mortise with a twybil.

Chisels and gouges

A tool with a narrow cutting edge capable of chopping out a mortise seems to have been a requirement from the earliest days. One solution was the mortise ax, which was pounded into the wood with a mallet. The French twybil had an unwieldy blade, up to 5ft (1.5m) in length, with a central handle and a cutting edge at each end. The twybil was swung to make short paring or chopping strokes and would only rarely have been struck with a mallet.

The more familiar pattern of chisel was also used for cutting stone and wood. The firmer chisel, with its stout rectangular-section blade, was the basic, general-purpose woodworking chisel and was designed to be struck with a mallet. It gradually evolved as carpenters and cabinetmakers required more specialized tools for paring, squaring mortises, inserting locks, and so on. The slick was a chisel 2 to 3ft (60 to 90cm) long, similar to the modern, two-handed Japanese paring chisel (see page 120).

As with our present-day tools, chisel blades were made with pointed tangs driven into wooden handles. Alternatively, the end of the handle was shaved to a point that fitted a hollow socket formed at the butt end of the blade.

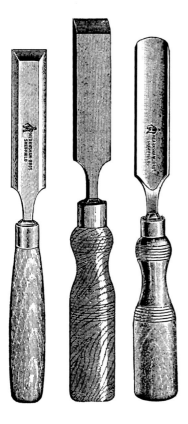

The joiner in the middle distance is cutting a mortise with a twybil.

MAKING FIXINGS

Until well into the nineteenth century, when it became possible to manufacture woodscrews cheaply, nailing was the preferred method for attaching one piece of wood to another. The first metal fittings made with helical screw threads were square-headed bolts turned with wrenches. Since the first slotted-head woodscrews appeared in the late sixteenth or early seventeenth centuries, the tools required to drive them into the wood must have been invented around the same time. Now known by the American term screwdrivers, these tools were originally called turnscrews.

Hammers

There's nothing new about hammers. Apart from the quality of manufacture, modern claw hammers are very similar to those used by medieval carpenters. The cross-peen hammer for "setting" small nails was developed in the early nineteenth century.

Screwdrivers

There was very little change in the design of screwdrivers until the invention of the spiral-ratchet screwdriver in the late 1890s and then, later still, the introduction of Phillips head screws.

BORING HOLES

At first sight, the modern-day bradawl would seem to employ what must have been the very first method used to bore a hole – pushing and twisting a pointed tool into the wood. But even this humble tool illustrates how woodworkers must have experimented with different methods in order to improve results. Merely forcing a sharp point into the wood pries the fibers apart, leading to a split along the grain which makes for a poor connection. The wedge-shape tip of a bradawl, when placed across the grain, severs the fibers as the awl is inserted; twisting the tool opens up a round hole.

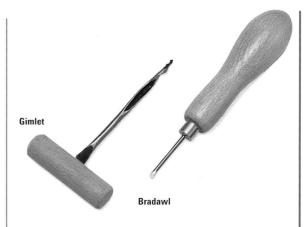

Gimlet

Bradawl

Gimlets and augers

The gimlet does a similar job to the bradawl, but it can cut deeper holes because it has a lead screw that pulls the tool into the wood and a spiral flute that removes waste wood. Augers are bigger versions of the gimlet, capable of boring large-diameter holes; considerable strength is required to drive the screw into the wood, then pull it out again to remove the waste.

Auger bits

Drills and braces

Mechanized tools for making holes included the bow drill and the pump drill, both of which employed a cord twisted around the "bit" to impart a reciprocating rotary motion. The carpenter's brace cranks the bit in one direction only. At first carpenters were forced to use a separate brace for each size of hole, but there were obvious advantages to be gained from a brace that could accommodate different-size bits. This was achieved by mounting metal bits in identical wooden blocks or "pads" that fitted into a tapered square hole cut in the end of the brace. Further improvements led to a brace with sprung pawls that engaged V-shape notches filed in the square tangs of special interchangeable bits. Wooden braces were attractive tools destined to become collectors' items, but they were bound to be replaced by the stronger and cheaper all-metal braces made from the middle of the nineteenth century.

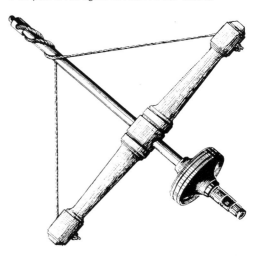

Reciprocating pump drill

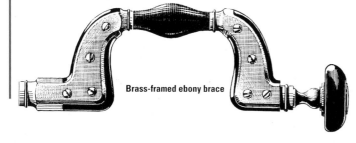

Brass-framed ebony brace

CHAPTER 2 "Measure twice, cut once" – sound advice which has no doubt saved many a young apprentice from the frustration of coming to assemble a project only to find that one or more components are the wrong size. But no matter how methodical you are, you cannot produce your best work with inaccurate or poorly maintained equipment, so buy only good-quality marking tools and treat them with care.

MARKING TOOLS

RULES AND TAPE MEASURES

Since even the best measuring tools are relatively inexpensive, most woodworkers acquire a variety of rules and tape measures to meet different needs. However, it is advisable to use the same rule or tape measure when marking out a project, just in case there is any variation between one tool and another. It generally makes sense to buy rules and tape measures that are made with both metric and imperial graduations – but take care not to confuse one system with the other once you have begun to mark out a workpiece. To ensure that several identical components are exactly the same size, measure one of them accurately, then use that piece of wood as a template to mark out the others.

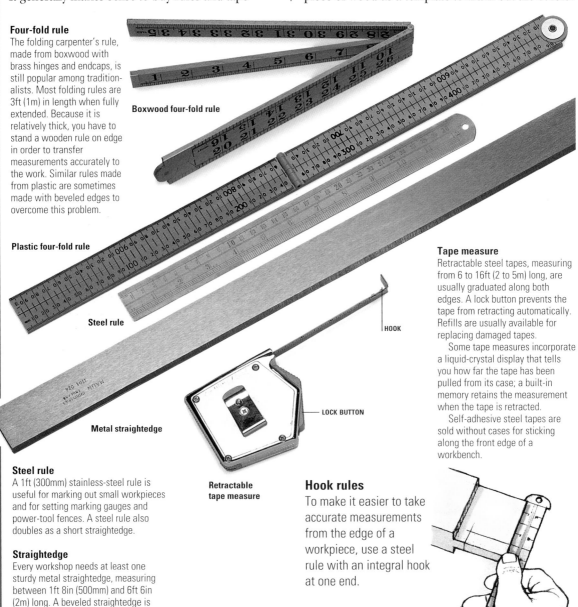

Four-fold rule
The folding carpenter's rule, made from boxwood with brass hinges and endcaps, is still popular among traditionalists. Most folding rules are 3ft (1m) in length when fully extended. Because it is relatively thick, you have to stand a wooden rule on edge in order to transfer measurements accurately to the work. Similar rules made from plastic are sometimes made with beveled edges to overcome this problem.

Boxwood four-fold rule

Plastic four-fold rule

Steel rule

Metal straightedge

Retractable tape measure

HOOK

LOCK BUTTON

Tape measure
Retractable steel tapes, measuring from 6 to 16ft (2 to 5m) long, are usually graduated along both edges. A lock button prevents the tape from retracting automatically. Refills are usually available for replacing damaged tapes.

Some tape measures incorporate a liquid-crystal display that tells you how far the tape has been pulled from its case; a built-in memory retains the measurement when the tape is retracted.

Self-adhesive steel tapes are sold without cases for sticking along the front edge of a workbench.

Steel rule
A 1ft (300mm) stainless-steel rule is useful for marking out small workpieces and for setting marking gauges and power-tool fences. A steel rule also doubles as a short straightedge.

Straightedge
Every workshop needs at least one sturdy metal straightedge, measuring between 1ft 8in (500mm) and 6ft 6in (2m) long. A beveled straightedge is ideal for making accurate cuts with a marking knife and for checking that a planed surface is perfectly flat. Some straightedges are etched with metric or imperial graduations.

Hook rules
To make it easier to take accurate measurements from the edge of a workpiece, use a steel rule with an integral hook at one end.

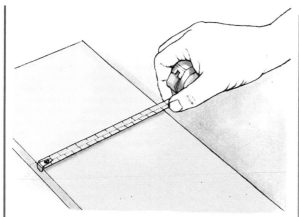

Measuring from edge to edge

When taking external measurements with a tape measure, hook the tip over one edge of the workpiece and read off the dimension against the opposite edge.

Taking internal measurements

When measuring between two components, the hook riveted to a retractable tape measure slides backward to align with the tip of the tape. Read off the dimension where the tape enters its case, then add the length of the case to arrive at the true measurement.

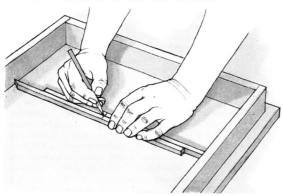

Using pinch rods

Another way to gauge the distance between components is to bridge the gap with two battens held side by side. Draw a mark across both battens to register their relative positions – then, without releasing your grip, transfer them to the work.

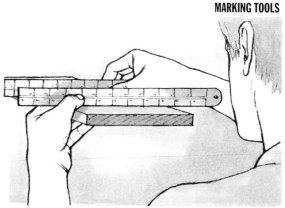

Checking for winding

If you suspect a board is twisted or "winding," hold a steel rule across each end; if the rules appear to be parallel, the board is flat.

Dividing a workpiece into equal parts

You can divide a workpiece into equal parts using any rule or tape measure. To divide a board into quarters, for example, align the tip of the rule with one edge and the fourth division with the opposite edge, then mark off the divisions between.

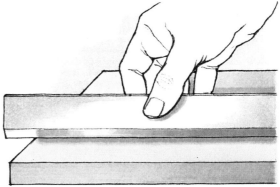

Checking a surface is flat

To check that a panel is flat, place a straightedge on the surface. A bump will cause the tool to rock; chinks of light showing beneath the straightedge indicate hollows. Turn the straightedge to various angles to gauge whether the entire surface is flat.

SQUARES AND BEVELS

Squares and sliding bevels are used by woodworkers to mark out workpieces and to check the accuracy of individual components and assemblies.

Try square
The finest try squares, used to mark and check right angles, have a blued-steel metal blade riveted at 90 degrees to a rosewood stock edged with brass. A square with a 1ft (300mm) blade is best for general woodwork, but you might find a smaller, all-metal engineer's square useful for fine work and for setting up power tools.

BLUED-STEEL BLADE

Miter square

ADJUSTABLE BLADE

Sliding bevel

LOCKING LEVER

ROSEWOOD STOCK

Try square

Miter square
Used for marking out and checking the accuracy of miter joints, the blade of a special-purpose miter square is fixed at 45 degrees to the stock.

Sliding bevel
A sliding bevel can be employed to mark or check any angle, using the adjustable blade which is secured with a short brass lever or wing nut.

Combination squares
Although dedicated miter and try squares are more accurate, you can buy a combination square that will serve both functions. Some try squares are made with the top inside corner of the stock cut at 45 degrees for marking out bevels, but an all-metal combination square with a sliding 1ft (300mm) blade is much more versatile. A knurled nut locks the blade in position, and most models have a spirit level built into the stock or head.

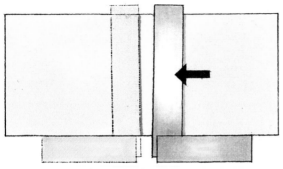

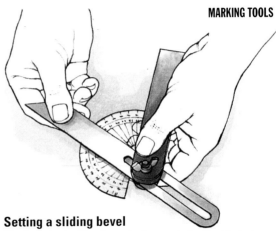

Checking the accuracy of a try square
From time to time, it pays to check the accuracy of your try square – this is especially important when using a combination square that does not have a fixed blade. Draw a line at right angles to the edge of a workpiece, turn the square over and slide the blade up to the marked line. The blade and the pencil mark will align precisely if the square is accurate.

Setting a sliding bevel
Slacken the locking lever just enough for the blade to move; set the required angle against a protractor, then retighten the lever.

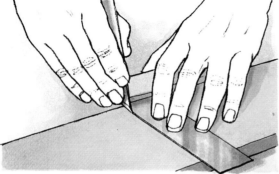

Marking with a try square
Mark out square shoulders with a try square. Use a pencil for the first stages of marking joints, but always use a marking knife, beveled on one side of the blade, to sever the wood fibers along lines that are to be sawn or chiseled.

Place the tip of the knife on the pencil line, and slide the square up to the flat side of the blade. Holding the square firmly against the face edge, draw the knife along the marked line.

Checking a miter or bevel
Place a miter square or sliding bevel over the beveled face of a workpiece. Keeping the blade in contact with the wood, slide the tool along the beveled face to check the angle is accurate across the width of the workpiece.

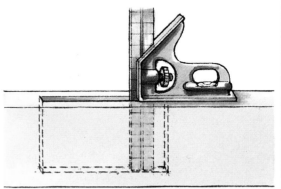

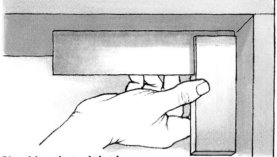

Checking that a joint is square
When assembling corner joints, use a try square to check that the two components meet at a right angle.

Using a square as a depth gauge
Measure the depth of a mortise with a combination square. Slacken the knurled nut, then place the tip of the blade against the bottom of the mortise and slide the head up against the edge of the work. Remove the tool and read the depth of the mortise against the inside edge of the head.

MARKING GAUGES

Gauges are designed to score fine lines parallel
with the edges of a workpiece, usually for marking
out joints or scribing rabbets.

Marking gauge
A marking gauge comprises an
adjustable fence or stock which
slides along a hardwood beam that
has a sharp steel pin driven through
one end. A thumbscrew clamps the
stock at any point along the
beam. Better-quality gauges
have brass strips set flush
with the running face of the
stock to prevent wear.

Mortise gauge
A mortise gauge is made with
two pins, one fixed and the
other adjustable, so
that you can score
both sides of a mortise
simultaneously. On the
best gauges the movable
pin is adjustable to very fine
tolerances, using a thumbscrew
located at the end of the beam.
Most mortise gauges have a
second fixed pin on the back of the
beam so that the tool doubles as a
standard marking gauge.

Cutting gauge
A cutting gauge is fitted with a
miniature blade instead of a
pointed pin, enabling you to
mark a line across the grain
without tearing the wood fibers.
The blade, which is held in place
with a brass wedge, can be
removed for sharpening. A
standard scribing blade,
used for marking various
corner joints, has a
rounded cutting tip.
Substitute a pointed knife-
edge blade for trimming
strips of veneer.

Curved-edge gauge
It is practically impossible to score
a line parallel to a curved edge
with an ordinary marking gauge.
A curved-edge gauge has a brass
fence that rests on two points,
preventing the stock from rocking
as it follows the edge of the work.
The same tool can also be used
on straight edges.

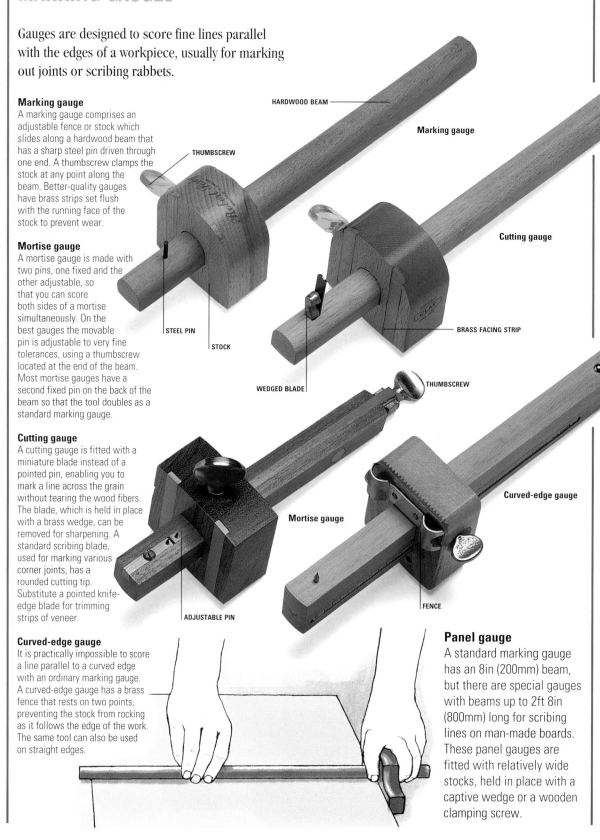

HARDWOOD BEAM

Marking gauge

THUMBSCREW

Cutting gauge

Marking gauge

STEEL PIN

STOCK

BRASS FACING STRIP

WEDGED BLADE

THUMBSCREW

Mortise gauge

Curved-edge gauge

FENCE

ADJUSTABLE PIN

Panel gauge
A standard marking gauge
has an 8in (200mm) beam,
but there are special gauges
with beams up to 2ft 8in
(800mm) long for scribing
lines on man-made boards.
These panel gauges are
fitted with relatively wide
stocks, held in place with a
captive wedge or a wooden
clamping screw.

1 Setting a marking gauge

Some marking gauges have graduated beams that make it easy to adjust the stock, but it is usually necessary to align the pin with a rule, then slide the stock with your thumb until it comes to rest against the end of the rule.

2 Adjusting a marking gauge

Tighten the thumbscrew and check the setting. If necessary, make fine adjustments by tapping the base of the beam against a bench to increase the distance between pin and stock. Reduce this distance by tapping the tip.

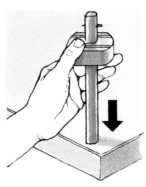

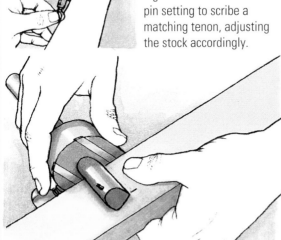

Setting a mortise gauge

Adjust the distance between the pins to match the width of a mortise chisel, then set the stock to suit the thickness of the leg or stile. Use the same pin setting to scribe a matching tenon, adjusting the stock accordingly.

Scribing with a gauge

Place the beam on the workpiece with the pin pointing towards you, then slide the stock up against the side of the work. Rotate the tool until the pin begins to mark the wood, then push the gauge away from you to scribe a clear line.

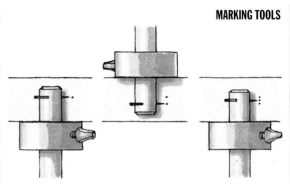

Gauging a center line

To find the exact center of a rail or stile, set a marking gauge as accurately as possible, then check the measurement by making a single pin prick, first from one side of the workpiece, then from the other. If the pin pricks fall short or overshoot the center line, adjust the gauge until they coincide.

IMPROVISING A GAUGE

For carpentry that does not require absolute precision, you can gauge lines with a pencil.

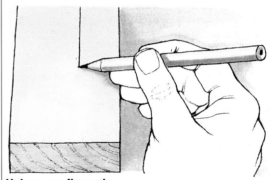

Using your fingertip

Run a fingertip against the edge of the workpiece to keep the pencil point on a parallel path.

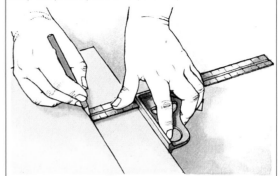

Gauging with a combination square

For slightly wider dimensions, follow the edge of the work with the head of a combination square, using the tip of the blade to guide the pencil point.

DIMENSIONING WOOD

As a prerequisite of any woodworking project, it is necessary to prepare the various components by cutting each piece of wood to size, ensuring that adjacent surfaces are planed flat and are at right angles to one another.

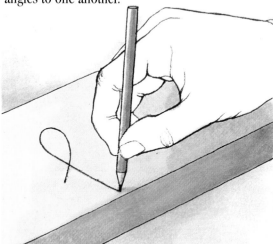

1 Selecting the face side
Choose what appears to be the most attractive and blemish-free face of a piece of wood, and plane it flat. Designate this planed surface as the "face side" by marking it with a loop that trails off to one edge.

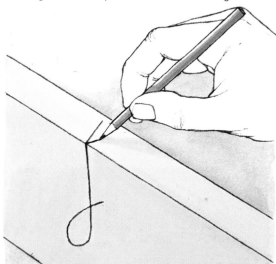

2 Planing the face edge
Plane this edge square to the face side. Check it with a try square, then mark it as the "face edge" by drawing an arrowhead pointing to the face-side loop. All other dimensions should now be measured and gauged from these two prepared surfaces.

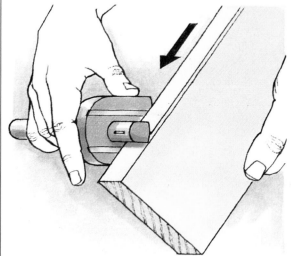

3 Planing to the required thickness
Set a marking gauge to the required thickness and scribe a line on both edges, working from the face side. Plane the unfinished surface down to these lines, checking that it is flat and square to the face edge.

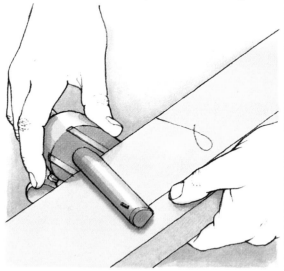

4 Cutting to width
Set the marking gauge to the required width of the workpiece, and scribe a line parallel with the face edge. Remove excess wood with a saw, finally planing down to the marked line. Check that this final edge is perfectly square.

CHAPTER 3 Whether they are made for fast cutting, designed to cut curved shapes, operated by hand or powered with electricity, all saws sever wood in basically the same way. Depending on the type of saw, its pointed teeth act like miniature chisels or knife blades, removing minute shavings or slivers of wood that fall to the floor as sawdust, leaving a slot or "kerf" that is slightly wider than the thickness of the saw blade.

HANDSAWS

Handsaws are designed for converting planks of solid wood and man-made boards into smaller components, ready for planing. The very best handsaws are skew-backed, having a gentle S-bend to the top of the blade which reduces the weight of the saw and improves its balance. The same blades are usually hollow ground, being reduced in thickness above the cutting edge to provide better clearance in the kerf.

Skew-backed, hollow-ground handsaw

Ripsaw

The largest handsaw, with a 2ft 2in (650mm) blade, is designed specifically for cutting solid wood in the direction of the grain. A ripsaw has large teeth with almost vertical leading edges, and each tooth is filed straight across to produce a chisel-like cutting tip. In common with all but the smallest saws, alternate teeth are "set," or bent to the right or left, to cut a kerf that is wider than the thickness of the blade. This prevents the saw from jamming in the wood. Ripsaws are made with 5 or 6 PPI (see opposite).

Ripsaw

Crosscut saw

A crosscut saw has teeth specially designed for severing solid wood across the grain, and is therefore the ideal saw for cutting planks of wood to length. Each tooth leans backward at an angle or "pitch" of 14 degrees, and is filed with a sharp cutting edge and tip that score the wood fibers on each side of the kerf. Crosscut-saw blades are between 2 to 2ft 2in (600 to 650mm) long, with 7 to 8 PPI.

Crosscut saw

Panel saw

Having relatively small crosscut teeth, at 10 PPI, a panel saw is designed primarily for cutting man-made boards to size, but doubles as a crosscut saw for severing solid wood. Panel-saw blades are between 1ft 8in and 1ft 10in (500 and 550mm) long.

Panel saw

Universal saw

Some manufacturers offer universal handsaws with teeth that are similar in shape to those of a crosscut saw but which cut well both with and across the grain. Universal saws are made with 6 to 10 PPI.

Dual purpose or fleam-tooth saws

These crosscutting saws are particularly efficient as they sever the wood on the return stroke as well as the forward. Fleam teeth have a pitch of 22.5 degrees.

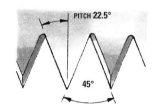

PITCH 22.5°

45°

Hardened saw teeth

Modern saws are sometimes subjected to a high-frequency hardening process. A hardpoint saw, which is distinguishable by its blue-black toothed edge, stays sharp longer than an untreated saw, but the metal is so hard that the teeth have to be sharpened by a specialist.

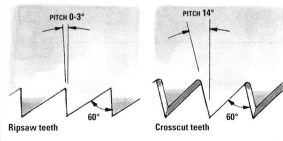

Ripsaw teeth   Crosscut teeth

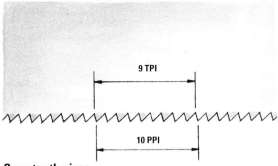

Saw-tooth sizes

Despite metrication, saw-tooth sizes are generally specified by the number of teeth that fit into 1 inch – TPI (teeth per inch) – measuring from the base of one tooth to the base of another. Alternatively, saw teeth may be specified by PPI (points per inch) counting the number of saw-tooth tips in 1 inch of blade. When compared, there is always one more PPI than TPI.

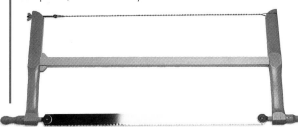

Frame saw

Although it resembles some curve-cutting saws (see page 37), a traditional-style frame saw is designed for ripping or crosscutting solid wood, depending on which blade is fitted. The narrow blade is held under tension by a twisted-wire tourniquet that runs between the solid-wood end posts or "cheeks". The frame can be swung to one side to provide clearance when ripping boards to width.

SAW HANDLES

Elegant handles are still made from tough short-grain hardwood, although the majority of handsaws now have molded plastic grips that are more economical to manufacture. The choice of material makes no difference to the performance of the saw, but be sure the handle feels comfortable to hold and check that it is set low behind the blade for maximum thrust on the forward stroke.

Open and closed grips

Some small dovetail saws and keyhole saws are made with open pistol-grip handles. However, most saws are made with stronger closed handgrips.

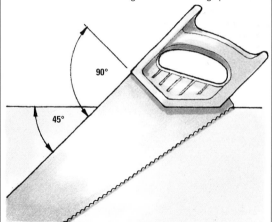

Using a saw as a square

Plastic handles are sometimes molded with shoulders set at 90 and 45 degrees to the straight back of the blade so that the saw can be used as a large try square or miter square.

Caring for handsaws

Saw teeth dull quickly if saws are thrown carelessly into a tool box or if one saw blade is dragged across another. Slip a plastic guard over the toothed edge of a blade before storing it, or carry your saws in a canvas case that is made with separate pockets to house a range of saws.

    Use turpentine to clean resin deposits from a saw blade, and wipe the metal with an oily rag before you put it away.

USING HANDSAWS

Provided the saw is sharp and the teeth have been set properly, it is possible to work for long periods with a handsaw without tiring.

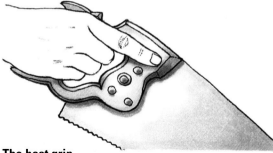

The best grip
Hold a handsaw with your forefinger extended towards the toe of the blade. This grip provides optimum control over the direction of cut and prevents the handle from twisting in the palm of your hand.

Starting the cut
Place the cutting edge of the saw just to the waste side of the marked line. Guiding the saw with your thumb held against the flat of the blade, make short backward strokes to establish the cut.

Following through
Saw with slow, steady strokes, using the full length of the blade – fast or erratic movements can be tiring, and the saw is more inclined to jam or wander off line.

   If the cut does begin to deviate from the intended course, twist the blade slightly to bring it back on line. If you find a saw consistently wanders, check that the teeth are set accurately.

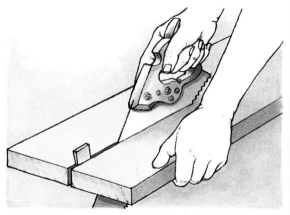

Prevent the saw from jamming
If the kerf begins to close on the blade, drive a small wedge into the cut to keep it open. Otherwise, lubricate the saw by rubbing a candle on both sides of the blade.

Finishing the cut
As you approach the end of a cut, lower the saw handle slightly and make slow, deliberate strokes as you sever the last few wood fibers. Support a long offcut with your free hand, or ask an assistant to take the weight while you finish sawing.

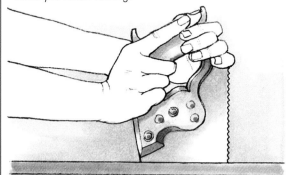

Reverse-action grip
To finish sawing a large panel or ripping a long plank of wood, turn round and saw back towards the kerf you have just made. Alternatively, use a two-handed grip to control the saw, continuing the kerf in the same direction but with the saw teeth facing away from you.

SUPPORTING THE WORK

You cannot hope to cut a workpiece with accuracy unless you support it properly. You can clamp a piece of wood to a bench top, but you may find it more comfortable to use a pair of trestles or "sawhorses" about 2ft (600mm) high, which will allow you to hold the work down with one hand and use your knee to keep it from swiveling.

Crosscutting
Bridge a pair of sawhorses with a plank of wood for crosscutting. If the workpiece is thin and whippy, support it from beneath with a thicker piece of wood. Clamp a short plank to the top of a single sawhorse.

Ripsawing
Support the work in a similar way when ripping a plank lengthwise, moving each sawhorse in turn to provide a clear path for the blade. Prevent a wide man-made panel from flexing by placing two planks under the board, one on each side of the kerf.

Crosscutting with a frame saw
When severing a plank of wood with a frame saw, cant the frame slightly to one side so that you can see the cut line clearly. Pass your free hand through the frame and behind the blade to support an offcut.

Ripping with a frame saw
Clamp the work to a sturdy bench, so that you can use two hands to control the saw, and turn the blade at 90 degrees to the frame. Grip one of the end posts with both hands, ensuring that the narrow blade cannot twist and cause the saw to wander off line.

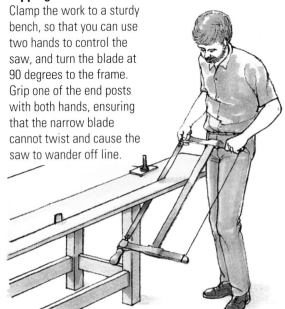

CIRCULAR SAWS

When fitted with the appropriate blades, a single electrically driven circular saw combines all the functions of a complete set of handsaws. A circular saw may be a trifle unwieldy for crosscutting smaller pieces of wood, but there is no disputing the fact that it is the ideal power tool for converting large numbers of solid-wood workpieces and full-size man-made panels.

Electric circular saws

A poorly made circular saw would be a dangerous tool, so choose a good-quality brand-name saw with a sturdy fence and blade guard. Check that the saw is well balanced and not too heavy, so you can work for prolonged periods without becoming tired. Some saws have built-in electronic systems that provide variable-speed control and supply additional power when the tool is under load. The initial kick that you normally feel when switching on a circular saw is also eradicated with electronic monitoring.

DUST-EXTRACTION PORT

HANDGRIP

TRIGGER

Handgrips
The main handgrip houses the trigger. A secondary handle mounted near the toe of the saw provides safe and positive control over the saw.

FIXED BLADE GUARD

DEPTH SCALE

MOTOR HOUSING

TILT SCALE

RETRACTABLE BLADE GUARD

BLADE

SECONDARY HANDLE

SIGHT FOR SAWING FREEHAND

FENCE CLAMP

SOLE PLATE

SIDE FENCE

Dust extraction
The fixed guard mounted above the blade is fitted with a dust-extraction port. This either deposits sawdust in a lightweight bag that can be emptied when full, or is connected directly to the hose of a portable dust extractor or industrial vacuum cleaner.

Safety lock
To prevent a saw from being switched on accidentally, a small button has to be depressed before the trigger will operate.

Insulating plastic body
All good power tools are made with non-conductive plastic casings to protect the user from electric shock.

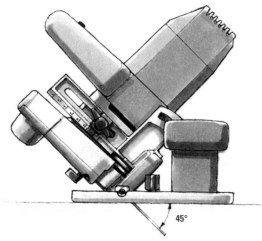

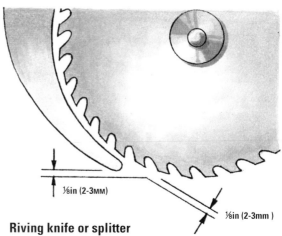

Blade-tilt facility

The sole plate of a circular saw can be adjusted to present the blade at any angle up to 45 degrees to the work surface. The angle is usually indicated on a quadrant scale; nevertheless, it pays to make a trial cut in scrap wood and to check the angle with a miter square or sliding bevel (see page 20).

Riving knife or splitter

Not a common feature of hand-held saws. This is the metal strip mounted directly behind the saw blade to prevent the kerf closing up. The riving knife should be adjusted to within ⅛in (2 to 3mm) of the saw teeth, and the tip of the knife should be about the same distance above the bottom edge of the blade.

Power rating

The power rating of a saw's electric motor is determined by what the manufacturer considers appropriate for the maximum size of blade that can be fitted. As a general rule, the larger the power rating for a given blade diameter, the better the saw's performance.

Blades

Circular saws can be fitted with a variety of blades, depending on the type of cut required and the material you are sawing (see page 32). On some saws clamping flanges on each side of the saw blade act as an anti-locking clutch, protecting the drive mechanism from damage by allowing the blade to slip if it becomes jammed in the work.

Fence

An adjustable side fence guides the blade on a path parallel to the edge of a workpiece.

Retractable guard

A circular saw is fitted with a retractable guard that is pushed back by the edge of the work as the blade is fed into the wood. A strong spring returns the guard, ensuring that the saw teeth are enclosed as soon as the blade is clear of the work. Before you use the saw, check that the guard is operating smoothly.

CORDLESS SAWS

A cordless saw is a convenient tool on remote work sites where there is no electrical service. However, batteries can only provide sufficient power for relatively short periods, and it is necessary to carry at least one spare battery pack.

Feed a cordless saw at a steady rate to avoid jamming the blade

CIRCULAR-SAW BLADES

Provided it is sharp, a good-quality circular-saw blade will make such a clean cut that the wood surface needs just a light skimming with a plane before sanding. Blades with tungsten-carbide-tipped teeth produce the best finish and stay sharp longer than ordinary blades. A PTFE (non-stick) coating reduces friction, increasing the life of the blade and the saw's drive mechanism. It also minimizes the risk of scorching the wood.

Top to bottom

Pointed-tooth blade
A blade designed primarily for crosscutting solid wood.

Fine-tooth blade
Intended for making fine cuts in chipboard and plastic-laminated panels. It cuts relatively slowly.

Ripsaw blade
A blade with large tungsten-carbide-tipped teeth and wide gullets that will clear the copious amounts of resinous sawdust created by ripping softwoods. It will also rip hardwoods and man-made boards, but is incapable of producing a first-class finish.

Chisel-tooth blade
A medium-priced, all-purpose saw blade suitable for ripping and crosscutting solid wood. It also copes with man-made boards.

Carbide-tipped universal saw
An excellent general-purpose saw blade for all solid wood and wood-based materials, including laminated boards. It leaves a fine finish when ripping or crosscutting softwood and hardwoods.

CHANGING A SAW BLADE

Always unplug a portable circular saw before changing a blade. When fitting a blade, check that the hole in the center is the right diameter for the saw's arbor (rotating shaft), and ensure that the teeth face away from the riving knife. Saw blades are attached with either nuts or allen screws.

Depth of cut

Blade size should not be confused with cutting depth. A 5in (130mm) blade, for example, will only cut to a maximum depth of about 1½in (40mm), considerably less than half its diameter. As a guide, the chart below illustrates maximum cutting depths of typical circular-saw blades. The maximum depth of cut is reduced when the blade is tilted for making beveled cuts.

Cutting depths of typical blades	
Blade diameter	Cutting depth
5in (130mm)	1½in (40mm)
6in (150mm)	1⅞in (46mm)
6½in (160mm)	2⅛in (54mm)
7½in (190mm)	2⅝in (66mm)
8½in (210mm)	3in (75mm)
9in (230mm)	3⅜in (85mm)

If you need a saw primarily for converting man-made boards, you may want to opt for one of the smaller models, especially as saws at the upper end of the scale can be cumbersome. At the very least, most woodworkers require a circular saw that can cut to a maximum depth of about 2in (50mm).

Adjusting the saw

Circular saws are adjusted for depth of cut by raising or lowering the body of the tool in relation to the sole plate. A depth scale is usually provided – but, as with most power-tool settings, it is often better to use the work itself as a guide when accuracy is important. Always unplug the saw before making adjustments.

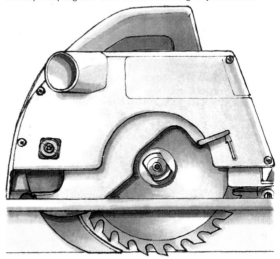

1 To sever the work

Withdraw the retractable guard and lay the sole plate on the work, with the blade resting against one edge. Release the clamp on the depth scale and lower the blade until the teeth project about ⅛in (2mm) below the work. Tighten the clamp before lifting the saw off the workpiece.

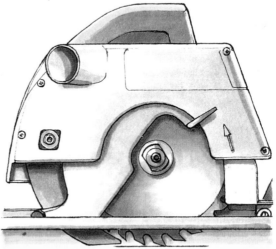

2 To make a partial cut

Mark the required cutting depth on the side of the workpiece, then adjust the blade until the saw teeth coincide with this mark.

USING A CIRCULAR SAW

The teeth of a circular saw move forward and upward when cutting, so any tearing of the grain will appear on the uppermost surface of the workpiece. Consequently, always lay the workpiece face-side down when ripping or crosscutting.

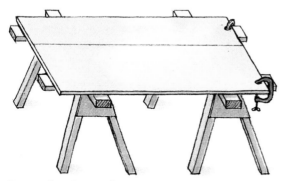

Supporting the work

Since you need both hands to control the saw, clamp the workpiece securely, either overhanging a bench top or to a pair of sawhorses. So that you can make one continuous pass with the saw, nail two stout battens across the top of the sawhorses, leaving a space between the battens for the saw blade. Whatever method you use to support the wood, check that there are no obstructions beneath the workpiece which might impede the safe passage of the blade.

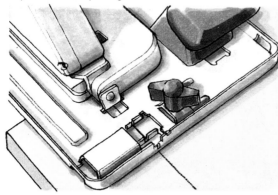

Sawing freehand

Circular saws have a small notch in the front edge of the sole plate which acts as a sight when cutting workpieces freehand.

Rest the front part of the sole plate on the work, aligning the notch with a cut line pencilled clearly on the wood. Switch on and feed the saw blade steadily into the work, following the marked line throughout the pass. Release the trigger and allow the retractable guard to snap closed before lifting the saw off the work.

Ripping with a fence

All saws can be fitted with an adjustable side fence to guide the blade on a path parallel to the edge of a workpiece. The fence can be mounted on either side of the saw and, although it should be sturdy enough as supplied, you can extend the fence by screwing a hardwood strip to its face.

Set the fence, using the scale marked on its mounting arm, then make a trial cut to check the setting before ripping the actual workpiece. Advance the saw into the wood at a steady rate, keeping the fence pressed against the edge of the workpiece.

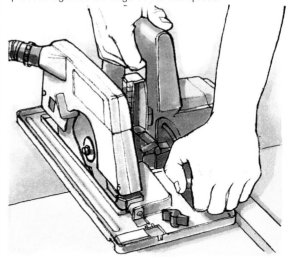

Crosscutting with a batten

When you need to make a cut across a wide board, run the edge of the sole plate against a straight batten clamped to the work. Most often the batten will be set at 90 degrees to the front edge, but you can clamp the batten to whatever angle is required. (See also MAKING A CROSSCUTTING T-SQUARE, opposite).

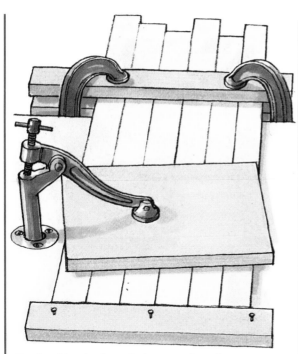

Cutting identical workpieces to length

To cut a number of workpieces to the same length, trim one end of each piece square and butt all the trimmed ends against a stop batten nailed or clamped to the bench. Clamp a guide batten across the workpieces and cut them all to length with one pass of the saw.

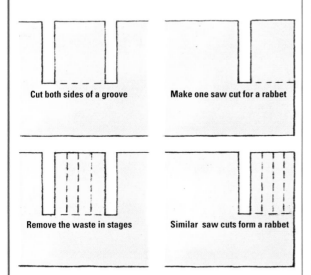

Cut both sides of a groove

Make one saw cut for a rabbet

Remove the waste in stages

Similar saw cuts form a rabbet

Cutting grooves and rabbets

Although it may not be the most obvious choice of tool, it is possible to cut grooves and rabbets with a circular saw. Set the fence to cut both sides of a groove or the inner edge of a rabbet, then reset the fence to remove the waste in stages.

MAKING A CROSSCUTTING T-SQUARE

Construct a T-square to use as a permanent guide for crosscutting boards.

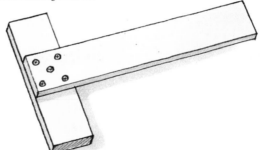

Making the T-square

Screw and glue a medium-density fiberboard straightedge to a solid-wood or MDF stock, checking that they form a perfect 90-degree angle.

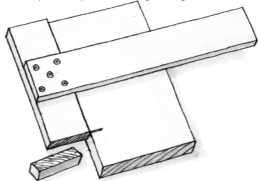

Cutting the stock to size

Clamp the T-square to a piece of scrap board and run the saw's sole plate against the straightedge to trim the end off the stock.

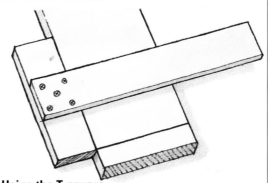

Using the T-square

When you want to use the T-square for crosscutting, hold the stock against the edge of the workpiece, aligning the trimmed end of the stock with a cut line marked across the wood or board. Clamp the straightedge to prevent the T-square from moving, and sever the workpiece on the waste side of the line with one pass of the circular saw.

BACKSAWS

Backsaws are made with relatively small crosscut teeth for trimming lengths of wood to size and for cutting woodworking joints. The special feature of all backsaws is the heavy steel or brass strip folded over the top of the blade. This strip of metal not only keeps the blade straight but provides sufficient weight to keep the teeth in contact with the wood without having to force the blade into the work.

Tenon saw
A tenon saw, having 13 to 15 PPI along a 10 to 14in (250 to 350mm) blade, is the largest and most versatile of the backsaw family. While it is possible to sever quite hefty sections of wood with a tenon saw, it is also a suitable saw for precise work such as cutting tenons and other large woodworking joints.

Dovetail saw
A dovetail saw is a smaller version of the tenon saw, but the teeth are too fine – 16 to 22 PPI – to be set conventionally, relying instead on the burr produced by file-sharpening (see page 101) to provide the extremely narrow kerf required for cutting dovetails and similar joints. Dovetail saws with traditional closed or pistol-grip handles are generally made with 8in (200mm) blades. An alternative-pattern saw, with a longer blade, has a straight handle in line with the folded metal strip.

Offset dovetail saw
A straight dovetail saw with a handle cranked to one side is made for trimming dowels and through tenons flush with the wood surface.

Bead saw
A miniature backsaw with about 26 PPI, the bead saw is ideal for cutting extremely fine joints and for model making.

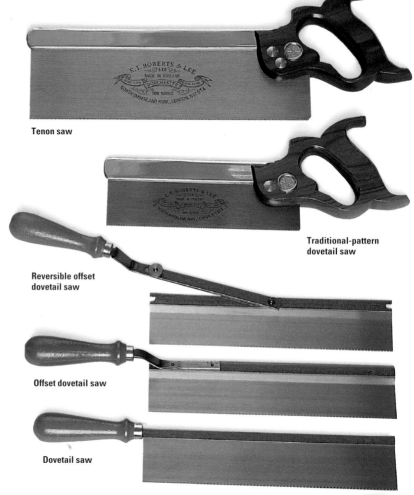

Tenon saw

Traditional-pattern dovetail saw

Reversible offset dovetail saw

Offset dovetail saw

Dovetail saw

Bead saw

Cutting with the grain
Clamp the work in a bench vise when sawing a tenon or dovetail down to the shoulder.

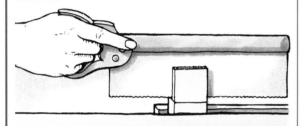

Crosscutting
Holding the work securely against a bench hook (see page 108), make short backward strokes on the waste side of the line until the cut is established; then gradually lower the blade to the horizontal as you extend the kerf.

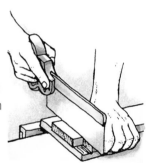

CURVE-CUTTING SAWS

A group of saws with narrow blades is made
specifically for cutting curved shapes or holes in
solid wood and boards. Various sizes and designs
are available; your choice will depend on the
material to be cut and the scale of the work.

Bow saw
A medium-weight frame saw
suitable for cutting relatively thick
pieces of wood, the bow saw is
fitted with an 8 to 12in (200 to
300mm) blade held under tension
by a tourniquet that runs between
the saw's end posts. The 9 to 17
PPI blades can be turned through
360 degrees to swing the frame
aside.

Coping saw
The very narrow blade of a 6in
(150mm) coping saw is held under
tension by the spring of its metal
frame. The 15 to 17 PPI blades are
too narrow to sharpen and are
simply replaced when they become
blunt or are broken. A coping saw
blade can be turned to swing the
frame out of the way to facilitate
cutting curves in either solid wood
or man-made boards.

Fret saw
Similar in construction to a coping
saw, the fret saw has a deep frame
that holds replaceable blades under
tension. A fret saw, with its 32 PPI
blades, is for cutting thin pieces of
wood and board or for shaping a
sandwich of marquetry veneers. A
fret saw cuts on the pull stroke to
prevent the blade from buckling.

Compass saw
Most curve-cutting saws are
limited by their frames to cutting
holes relatively close to the edges
of a workpiece. A compass saw
has a narrow, tapered blade that is
stiff enough to hold its shape
without being held under tension
and, as a result, can be used to cut
a hole in a board of any thickness
as far from the edges as required.
The 8 to 10 PPI blades are either
bolted into a pistol-grip handle or
fitted into a straight handle which
is convenient for turning the saw
to cut in any direction.

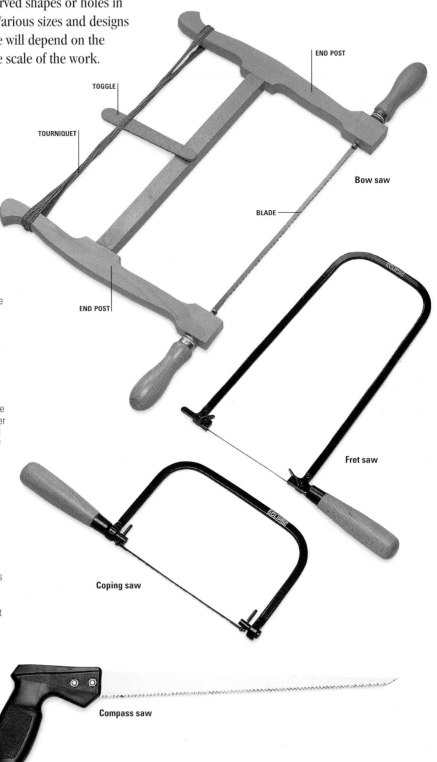

END POST

TOGGLE

TOURNIQUET

Bow saw

BLADE

END POST

Fret saw

Coping saw

Compass saw

PISTOL-GRIP HANDLE

USING CURVE-CUTTING SAWS

Most curve-cutting saws require special techniques to counter the tendency for the weight of their frames to turn the blade off line.

Using a fret saw
Thin workpieces tend to vibrate unless they are supported from below by a strip of plywood screwed to the bench top, overhanging the front edge. Cut a V-shape notch in the plywood to provide clearance for the fret-saw blade. So that you can cut downwards on the pull stroke, sit on a low stool with your chest at about bench height.

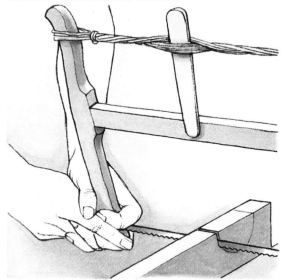

Cutting with a bow saw
A bow saw requires a two-handed grip to control the direction of cut and compensate for the twisting force of the frame. Grip the straight handle with one hand, extending your forefinger in line with the blade. Place your free hand alongside the other, wrapping the forefinger and middle finger around the saw's end post, one on each side of the blade.

Making closed cuts
When cutting a hole with any frame saw, mark out the work and bore a small access hole for the blade, just inside the waste. Pass the saw blade through the hole and connect it to the frame.

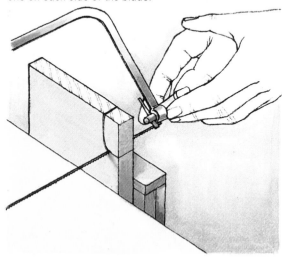

Controlling a coping saw
To prevent the blade from wandering off line, place the first joint of your extended forefinger on the coping saw's frame. If it feels more comfortable, close your other hand around the first to form a double-handed grip.

Sawing holes with a compass saw
When cutting holes with a compass saw, drill a starter hole for the tip of the blade. Saw steadily to avoid buckling the blade on the forward stroke.

REPLACING BLADES

Curve-cutting saws are designed for quick and easy replacement of blunt, broken or bent blades.

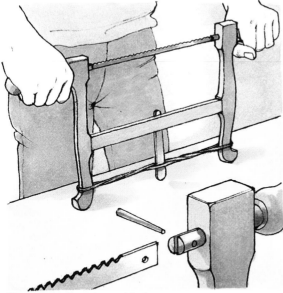

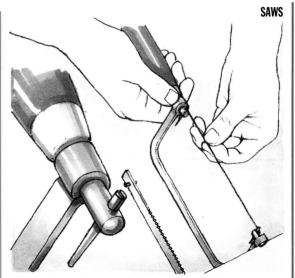

Changing a bow-saw blade
Unwind the toggle to slacken the tourniquet, then locate each end of the blade in the slotted metal rods that extend from the handles. Pass the tapered retaining pins through the rods and blade at both ends. Tighten the tourniquet again and rotate both handles to straighten the blade.

Replacing a damaged coping-saw blade
Each end of a coping-saw blade fits into a slotted retaining pin. To replace a damaged blade, reduce the distance between the retaining pins by turning the saw's handle counterclockwise; hold the pin attached to the handle between finger and thumb to prevent it from spinning.

Attach the blade to the toe of the saw, with the teeth facing away from the handle. Flex the frame against the edge of a bench until you can locate the other end of the blade. Holding its retaining pin as before, tighten the handle to tension the blade; then align both pins by eye.

Fitting a compass-saw blade
To fit a compass-saw blade, slacken the screw bolts and slide the slotted end of the replacement blade into the handle. Tighten both bolts.

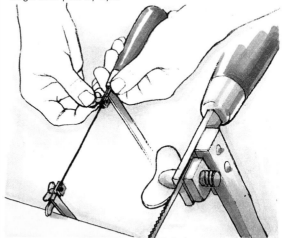

Fitting a fret-saw blade
Fret-saw blades are fitted in a similar way, but instead of retaining pins a thumbscrew clamps the flat section at each end of a blade. With the teeth facing the handle, clamp the toe end of the blade, then flex the frame against a bench, tightening the other thumbscrew onto the blade. Releasing pressure on the frame is sufficient to put the blade under tension.

SABRE SAWS

Though you can make straight cuts using a side fence or straightedge as a guide, you only really begin to appreciate the advantages of a power sabre saw when you come to cut curves and apertures – tasks it can perform effortlessly whether sawing through solid wood or man-made boards. With the right blade, you can even saw through sheet metal and plastics.

Power sabre saws

When you buy a portable sabre saw these days, you get a lot for your money. Variable speed control and pendulum action are more or less standard, and many saws incorporate electronics that regulate the saw's performance for optimum effect. Fitted with dust extraction and electric motors that can run continuously for long periods with very little noise or vibration, well-made power sabre saws are comfortable to use and easy to control.

Motor size
Power sabre saws are fitted with precisely balanced ½ to ¾ HP (350 to 600W) electric motors, capable of a maximum speed of about 3000 strokes per minute. Larger motors are intended for cutting thicker material rather than to produce a higher stroke rate.

Trigger lock
When making long or complicated cuts, switch on and depress the trigger-lock button to keep the saw running continuously. Switch off again by squeezing the trigger.

Dust extraction
Sawdust constitutes a health risk and a fire hazard, so either fit a dust-collecting bag to your sabre saw or attach a flexible hose between the saw's exhaust port and an industrial vacuum cleaner that will suck up the dust as soon as it is created.

STROKE-RATE SELECTOR

TRIGGER-LOCK BUTTON

TRIGGER

BLADE GUARD

BLADE

PENDULUM-ACTION SELECTOR

SHOE

DUST-EXHAUST PORT

BOSCH PST 60 PEA
380W · max 60 mm · electronic

Power sabre saw

Pendulum action

As well as moving the saw blade up and down, sabre saws with pendulum or orbital action also cause the blade to cut faster by moving the blade forward into the work on the upstroke and help clear sawdust from the kerf by moving the blade backward on the downstroke. Select maximum advance for softwood and plastics, gradually reducing the degree of oscillation for hardwoods, chipboard and soft metals. Select zero movement for steel and to prevent thin sheet materials from vibrating.

Depth of cut

The average power sabre saw will cut wood up to 2¾in (70mm) thick, non-ferrous metals up to ¾in (18mm) thick, and sheet steel up to ⅛in (3mm) thick.

Speed selection

Basic sabre saws run at high speed the whole time, but the majority of saws have some form of speed control that permits you to select the optimum stroke rate for the material you are cutting. This may take the form of a dial that allows you to pre-select from a range of speeds from 500 to 3000 strokes per minute – but on a true variable-speed sabre saw the speed is controlled by how much pressure you apply to the trigger (though this too can be limited to a particular stroke rate, usually by means of a built-in dial). In general, it is best to select the higher speeds for woodworking and the middle range for aluminum and plastics, reserving the lowest stroke rates for cutting sheet steel or ceramic tiles. Constant-speed electronics monitor the stroke rate, maintaining the selected speed within reasonable limits to cope with changes in the feed rate and density of the material being cut.

Bevel-cutting facility

The metal shoe (sole plate) of an electric sabre saw can be tilted to any angle up to 45 degrees for cutting bevels.

Electrical insulation

Nearly all power sabre saws are manufactured with non-conductive plastic casings to protect users from electric shock.

Splinter control

The reciprocal action of a sabre saw blade tends to splinter the kerf on the upper surface of a workpiece. The shoe on some saws can be adjusted fore-and-aft to locate the blade within a narrow slot in the metal. This reduces the clearance on each side of the blade, minimizing breakout along the kerf. The same thing is achieved on other saws by fitting a plastic insert that surrounds the blade.

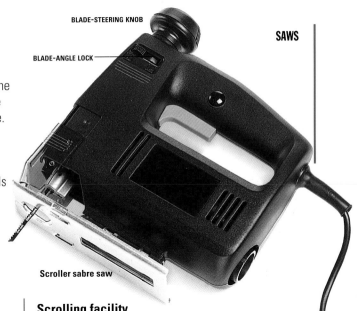

BLADE-STEERING KNOB

BLADE-ANGLE LOCK

Scroller sabre saw

Scrolling facility

With a scroller sabre saw, the blade can be steered independently so that you can follow a curve with the cutting edge without having to reorient the saw itself or adjust the position of the work. A knob on top of the saw controls the direction of the blade, which can be locked facing forward, backward or sideways for convenience. Even with a scroller saw, it is still vital to keep the pressure directly behind the cutting edge, or the blade will break.

CORDLESS SABRE SAWS

Very few battery-operated sabre saws are manufactured for the amateur woodworking market, although the advantage of a curve-cutting saw without a trailing cord is obvious. However, you need to recharge a cordless saw after a relatively short period of continuous running, especially when cutting dense materials such as chipboard. Consequently, it pays to have a spare battery on hand at all times.

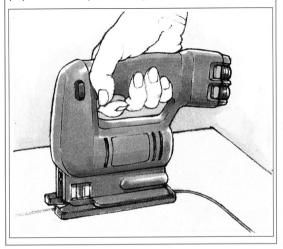

SABRE SAW BLADES

Different types of sabre saw blade are available for cutting a variety of materials. Blades are also designed to cut faster, cleaner, or to make particularly tight turns.

Top to bottom:
Side-set wood blade
Especially good for cutting softwoods and hardwoods with the grain. It produces a fairly rough cut.

Ground and side-set blade
As above, but produces a cleaner cut.

Ground wood blade
Ideal blade for making very clean cuts in solid wood and man-made boards.

Wavy-set blade
Makes a very fine kerf when cutting man-made boards.

Narrow wavy-set blade
For cutting tight curves in wood and man-made boards.

Reverse-tooth blade
Cuts on the down stroke to prevent chipping of plastic-laminated boards.

Tungsten-carbide tipped
Excellent for chipboard and other boards manufactured with a high glue content.

Wood file
Half-round, flat and triangular files are available for fitting in a power sabre saw.

Ground-metal blade
For cutting nonferrous metals, such as aluminum.

Side-set metal blade
Made from high-speed steel, this blade cuts nonferrous metals and mild steel.

Wavy-set metal blade
As above, but for thin sheet metal only.

For GRP and ceramics
Tungsten-carbide-coated for cutting glass-reinforced plastic and ceramic tiles.

Knife-ground blade
Cuts soft rubber, cardboard, cork, plastics and carpet.

Blade length
Blade size is specified according to the length of the cutting edge. For the most part, you will be using just the top section of a blade, but make sure that any blade you buy for a specific task is at least ⅝ to ¾in (15 to 18mm) longer than the maximum thickness of the wood you intend to saw.

Size of teeth
As with most saw blades, sabre saw-tooth size is specified as teeth per inch (TPI) or sometimes using the engineering term "pitch," which describes the distance in millimeters between the point of one tooth and another. For example, the same blade could be described as having 10 TPI or a pitch of 2.5mm.

Set of tooth
Sabre saw-blade teeth are sometimes side set in the conventional manner – alternate teeth being bent to the right and left. For making finer cuts, the teeth are not set but the blade is ground to a thinner section behind the row of teeth to provide a clearance in the kerf. And blades with extremely fine teeth are wavy set, that is, with a serpentine cutting edge that produces a wider kerf than the true thickness of the blade.

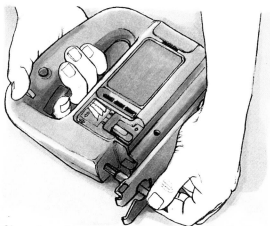

Changing a blade
Sabre saw blades are never sharpened; they are simply discarded when they break or become blunt. Consequently, all sabre saws are designed for easy blade replacement. Blades are held in place by a clamp that is operated by hand, using a special key, or the saw has a built-in clamp-release mechanism. Follow the manufacturer's instructions for changing a blade, checking that the roller guide is supporting the blade from behind. Unplug the saw when changing blades.

USING A SABRE SAW

When cutting with a sabre saw, clamp the work so that it overhangs the edge of a bench or bridges a pair of sawhorses. Unless it is held firmly, thin sheet material, in particular, will vibrate and throw the blade off course. Make sure that the cord from an electrically driven sabre saw trails behind the blade and cannot get caught up on an obstruction as you feed the saw across the workpiece surface.

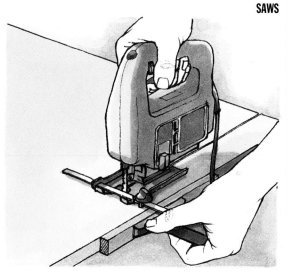

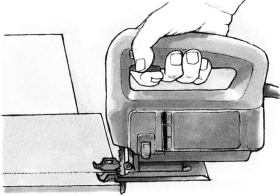

Sawing freehand
Rest the front of the shoe on the work, aligning the blade with a line marked on the work. Switch on and feed the blade steadily into the work. Follow the line, maintaining a constant feed rate without forcing the pace. Relieve the pressure on the blade as you approach the end of the marked line to avoid a sudden acceleration as you finally sever the offcut. Switch off and let the blade come to rest before you put the saw down.

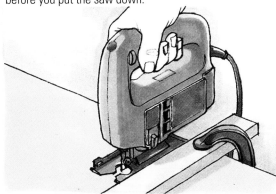

Using a straightedge
Since it is practically impossible to follow a straight line accurately when sawing freehand, run the saw's shoe against a wooden straightedge clamped across the work. Maintain side pressure against the straightedge as you continue to feed the blade at a steady rate.

Sawing parallel to an edge
When the intended line of cut is close to the edge of a workpiece, you can fit a side fence to the saw. Because these fences are comparatively short, a longer hardwood strip screwed to the fence face will help keep the blade on course.

To set the fence, align the blade with the marked line (as described left), then slide the fence up against the guide edge and tighten the fence clamp. Keep the fence pressed against the guide edge while feeding the saw through the work; make sure you do not curl your fingers around the edge of the work near the line of cut. If the saw consistently wanders off line, check that the blade is accurately set parallel to the fence face.

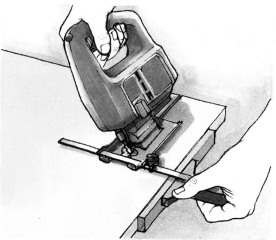

Cutting bevels
Use a guide fence or a straightedge to guide the saw when making beveled cuts. To adjust the angle of the blade, slacken the shoe clamping screws and tap the shoe with a screwdriver handle until the required angle is indicated on the saw's tilt gauge. Retighten the clamps and make a test cut to check the setting.

CUTTING HOLES AND CURVES

Most gentle curves can be followed freehand (see page 43), but you may need to attach accessories to the sabre saw or use straight guide battens to help you cut perfectly circular holes or large rectangular apertures.

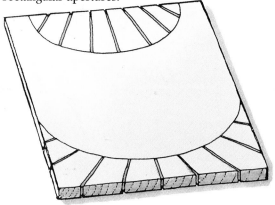

Making curved cuts
Forcing a blade around a tight bend will result in the blade breaking or the edge of the work being scorched. To relieve the blade in a tight kerf, make a series of straight cuts through the waste up to the marked line. As you proceed with cutting the curve, the waste will fall off in sections, providing sufficient clearance for the blade.

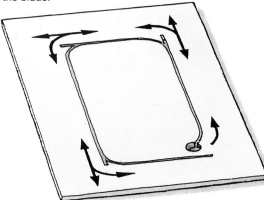

Cutting a rectangular aperture
When cutting an aperture with rounded corners, drill a starter hole in the waste, then lower the blade into the hole and make one continuous pass with the saw.

To cut an aperture with square corners, feed the blade into each corner in turn, back off about 1in (25mm) and cut a curve that intercepts the next straight section. When you have cut all four sides, turn the sabre saw around and saw back into each corner from the opposite direction to sever the remaining waste.

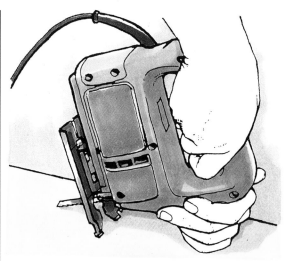

Plunge cutting with a sabre saw
Plunge cutting, a technique that requires a little practice to perfect, saves you having to drill starter holes when sawing apertures in man-made boards. Tip the saw onto the front edge of its shoe, with the blade held clear of the work. Switch on and gradually pivot the saw on the shoe until the point of the blade cuts its way through the wood. Once the shoe is flat on the work, continue to saw in the normal way. Always plunge-cut well within the waste wood and not too close to the marked lines.

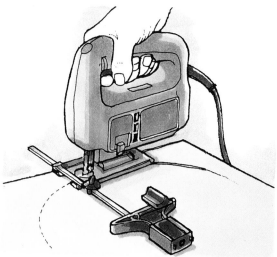

Cutting circles
To cut a perfectly circular aperture, convert your side fence into a trammel, using a detachable point supplied with the accessory. Press the point into the center of the waste wood, and pivot the saw about it. If you want to cut a disk instead of a hole, press the trammel point into a small patch of plywood stuck over the center of the disk with double-sided adhesive tape.

CHAPTER 4 The primary function of a basic plane is to remove saw marks, leaving the surface of the wood perfectly smooth. If required, workpieces can be planed square at the same time. A spokeshave is used similarly, but for smoothing and shaping curved edges. In addition, there are a great many specialized planes designed specifically for cutting rabbets, grooves and a variety of moldings.

BENCH PLANES

The basic bench plane is available in a range of sizes, providing the woodworker with the means to smooth workpieces of various lengths and widths.

The replaceable-blade bench plane is a relatively new concept. When blunt, its narrow cutter is discarded and a new one substituted.

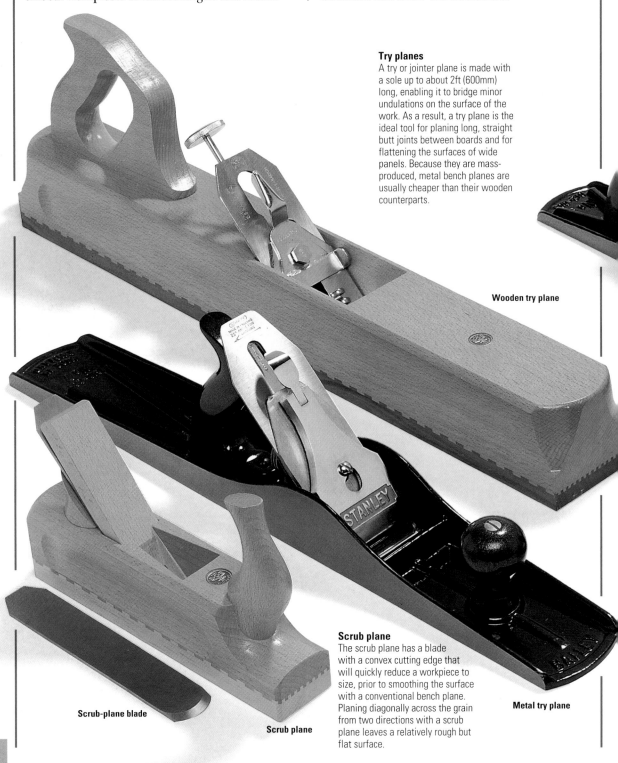

Try planes
A try or jointer plane is made with a sole up to about 2ft (600mm) long, enabling it to bridge minor undulations on the surface of the work. As a result, a try plane is the ideal tool for planing long, straight butt joints between boards and for flattening the surfaces of wide panels. Because they are mass-produced, metal bench planes are usually cheaper than their wooden counterparts.

Wooden try plane

Scrub-plane blade

Scrub plane

Scrub plane
The scrub plane has a blade with a convex cutting edge that will quickly reduce a workpiece to size, prior to smoothing the surface with a conventional bench plane. Planing diagonally across the grain from two directions with a scrub plane leaves a relatively rough but flat surface.

Metal try plane

Jack plane
With its 1ft 3in (380mm) long sole, the jack plane is a good general-purpose plane, long enough to make reasonably accurate edge joints but not so unwieldy that it cannot be used to finish most workpieces square and flat.

Smoothing plane
The relatively short smoothing plane is used to take very fine shavings as a means of producing the final planed surface on a workpiece. The best wooden smoothing planes have self-lubricating lignum vitae soles.

Replaceable-blade bench plane

Metal jack plane

Wooden jack plane

Metal smoothing plane

Wooden smoothing plane
with lignum vitae sole

47

DISMANTLING AND ADJUSTING BENCH PLANES

All metal bench planes are made with similar components and are dismantled in the same way. In some planes, the blade is held in place with a wedge, although most modern planes made from wood are fitted with capped blades and depth-adjustment screws.

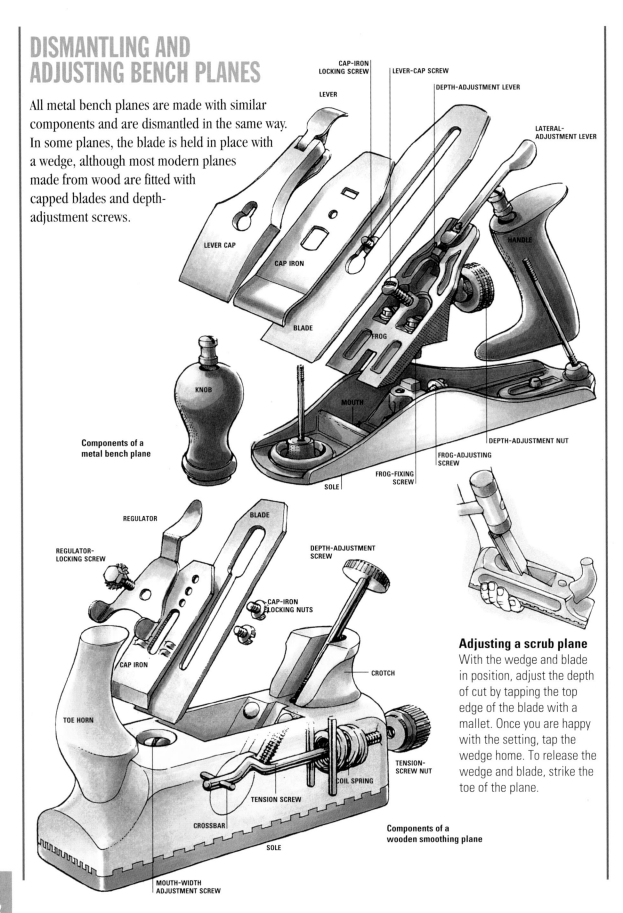

CAP-IRON LOCKING SCREW

LEVER

LEVER-CAP SCREW

DEPTH-ADJUSTMENT LEVER

LATERAL-ADJUSTMENT LEVER

LEVER CAP

CAP IRON

HANDLE

BLADE

FROG

KNOB

MOUTH

Components of a metal bench plane

DEPTH-ADJUSTMENT NUT

FROG-ADJUSTING SCREW

FROG-FIXING SCREW

SOLE

REGULATOR

BLADE

DEPTH-ADJUSTMENT SCREW

REGULATOR-LOCKING SCREW

CAP-IRON LOCKING NUTS

CAP IRON

CROTCH

TOE HORN

Adjusting a scrub plane
With the wedge and blade in position, adjust the depth of cut by tapping the top edge of the blade with a mallet. Once you are happy with the setting, tap the wedge home. To release the wedge and blade, strike the toe of the plane.

TENSION-SCREW NUT

COIL SPRING

CROSSBAR

TENSION SCREW

Components of a wooden smoothing plane

SOLE

MOUTH-WIDTH ADJUSTMENT SCREW

Removing the blade and cap iron

In order to remove the blade for sharpening or to make other adjustments to a metal bench plane, first take off the lever cap by lifting its lever and sliding the cap backward to release it from its locking screw. Lift the blade and cap iron out of the plane, revealing the wedge-shaped casting known as the "frog," which incorporates the blade-depth and lateral-adjustment controls.

To separate the cap iron and blade, use a large screwdriver to loosen the locking screw, then slide the cap iron towards the cutting edge until the screw head can pass through the hole in the blade.

Adjusting the frog

The cutting edge of the blade protrudes through an opening in the sole called the mouth. By adjusting the frog, you can modify the size of this opening to suit the thickness of the wood shavings you want to remove. When you are coarse planing, for example, open the mouth to provide adequate clearance for thick shavings. Close the mouth when taking fine shavings, to encourage them to break and curl against the cap iron.

To slide the frog forward or backward, release its two fixing screws, then turn the frog-adjusting screw with a screwdriver.

Removing the blade from a wooden plane

Back-off the depth-adjustment screw by about ½in (10mm), and loosen the tension-screw nut at the heel of the plane. Turn the tension screw's crossbar through 90 degrees to release the blade assembly, which includes the cap iron and regulator. To dismantle the assembly for sharpening, remove the two screws at the back of the blade.

Assembling and adjusting a wooden plane

Having sharpened the blade (see pages 96–7), replace the cap iron and lower the assembly into the plane. Pass the crossbar through the slot in the assembly, turning the bar to locate it in its seat in the cap iron, then slightly tighten the tension-screw nut.

Adjust the depth screw until the blade protrudes through the mouth of the blade and use the regulator to ensure the cutting edge is parallel with the sole. Back off the depth adjuster to the required setting and finally tighten the tension-screw nut.

To open or close the mouth on a wooden plane, adjust the screw behind the toe horn.

ASSEMBLING A METAL-PLANE BLADE AND CAP IRON

Having sharpened the blade, replace the cap iron and insert the assembly in the plane before making the necessary adjustments.

1 Placing the cap iron on the blade
Holding the blade bevel-downwards, lay the cap iron across it and locate the head of the captive locking screw in the hole in the blade.

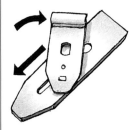

2 Aligning cap iron and blade
Sliding the screw along the slot in the blade, swivel the cap iron until it aligns with the blade. Don't drag the cap iron across the cutting edge.

3 Sliding iron forward
Slide the cap iron to within ⅟₁₆in (1mm) or less of the cutting edge and tighten the locking screw.

4 Inserting the blade assembly
Lower the blade assembly into the plane, fitting it over the projecting lever-cap screw and onto the stub of the depth-adjustment lever. Replace the lever cap.

5 Adjusting the blade
Turn the depth-adjust-ment nut until the blade protrudes from the mouth. Looking along the sole from the toe of the plane, move the lateral-adjust-ment lever until the cutting edge appears to be parallel with the sole. Set the depth of cut.

SERVICING BENCH PLANES

You may experience minor difficulties from time to time but, provided you take reasonable care of your bench planes, they should require very little servicing except for sharpening. Keep planes clean and well lubricated, and occasionally wipe exposed metal surfaces with an oily rag. Store bench planes on their sides, with their blades withdrawn.

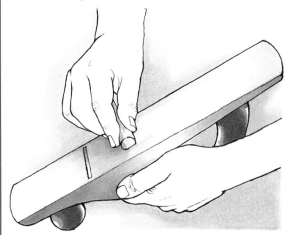

Lubricating a sticky sole
Wooden planes tend to become slick with regular use and rarely require any form of lubrication. However, if you feel that a metal plane is not gliding across the work as it should, lightly rub a stub of white candle across the sole.

Correcting blade chatter
If your plane vibrates or "chatters," instead of taking a shaving smoothly, check that the blade is held securely. Tighten the lever-cap screw or, if you are using a wooden plane, the tension-screw nut.

If the fault persists, check that there are no foreign bodies trapped behind the blade and, in the case of a metal bench plane, tighten the frog's fixing screws.

Preventing shavings from jamming under the cap iron
Shavings get caught between the leading edge of the cap iron and the blade when these are not fitting snugly against one another. Check that the back of the blade is perfectly flat and that there are no deposits of resin which would prevent the cap iron from bedding down. If the blade is bent, lay it on a flat board and strike it firmly with a hammer.

Re-dress the leading edge of the cap iron on an oilstone, taking care to hone the edge flat and at the original angle.

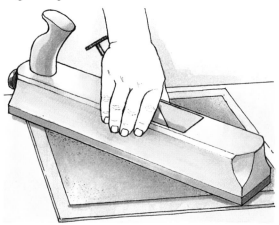

Flattening a warped sole
If your plane seems incapable of taking a thin shaving, lay a metal straightedge across the sole to check that it is not warped. You can correct a warped metal plane by rubbing its sole on a sheet of emery paper or cloth held down on a piece of thick glass with double-sided adhesive tape. However, before undertaking such a long, laborious process, it is worth checking whether you can have the plane reground by a professional.

Flattening a wooden sole on abrasive paper is much easier. Remove the blade and, holding the plane near its center, rub the sole back and forth across the paper, checking it regularly with a straightedge.

USING BENCH PLANES

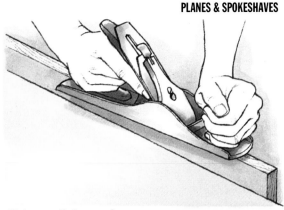

When setting up a workpiece for planing, inspect the wood to ascertain the general direction of the grain. Planing with the grain is always preferable, since planing in the opposite direction tends to tear the wood fibers. If you are planing wood with irregular grain, adjust the plane to take very fine shavings. See page 55 for planing end grain.

Handling a metal plane
Grasp the handle of a metal bench plane with your forefinger extended towards the toe of the tool – this guarantees control over the direction of the plane. Place your free hand on the round knob to hold the toe down on the work.

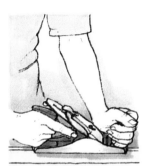

Handling a wooden smoothing plane
Nestle your hand into the shaped crotch just above the heel of the plane, grasping the body with your fingers and thumb. Use the ergonomic horn to provide downward pressure.

Using a slicing action
It is sometimes easier to smooth irregular grain if you create a slicing action by turning the plane at a slight angle to the direction of travel.

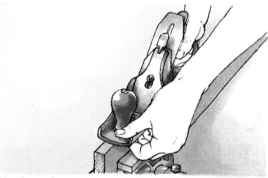

Planing edges
Maintain a square edge by putting pressure on the toe with your thumb, curling your fingers under the plane to act as a guide fence against the side of the work. Use a similar grip to hold the plane at an angle when planing chamfers along a workpiece.

The planing action
Stand beside the bench with your feet apart, your rear foot pointing towards the bench, and the other parallel with it. With your feet firmly planted, move your upper body to propel the plane forward. Keep the weight on the toe of the plane as you begin the stroke, transferring pressure to the heel to prevent the plane from rounding off the work at the far end.

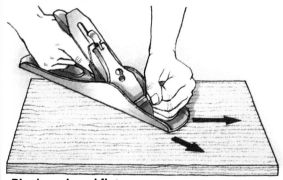

Planing a board flat
To plane a board flat, begin by planing at a slight angle across it from two directions. Check the surface with a straightedge (see page 19), then adjust the plane to take thinner shavings and finish with strokes parallel to the edges of the workpiece.

POWER PLANERS

A portable planer cannot do the work of a finely set hand plane, nor can it take the place of a stand-alone planer/thicknesser, but it does reduce the work involved in planing large sections of wood to size and is a boon to carpenters who need to skim the closing edge of a door or plane a beveled rabbet on a hardwood windowsill.

Handgrip
The weight of the tool is taken with the main handgrip. This also incorporates the trigger and the lock button, which when depressed allows the machine to run continuously. Before you plug it in, check that the planer is not locked for continuous running.

Secondary handle
A secondary handle mounted above the toe helps to control the planer. This secondary handle often doubles as the cutting-depth adjuster. Always use the handgrip and handle to control the tool; never curl your fingers around the edge of the sole.

LOCK BUTTON

EXHAUST PORT

SECONDARY HANDLE

HANDGRIP

TRIGGER

BOSCH
PHO 2-82
600 W
Drehzahl/No load/Tr. à vide | 1/min | 13000
Hobelbreite/Planing width/
Largeur de rabotage | mm | 82
Falztiefe/Rabbeting depth/
Epaisseur de feuillure | mm | 20
Spantiefe/Planing depth/
Epaisseur des copeaux | mm | 0-2

CUTTING-DEPTH DIAL

RABBET-DEPTH GAUGE

ADJUSTABLE FENCE

SOLE

Portable power plane

Dust extractor
While the machine is running, it ejects a considerable amount of shavings from its exhaust port. It pays to catch them in an appropriate bag or, better still, to attach a flexible hose connected to an industrial vacuum cleaner.

Insulation
A plastic, double-insulated casing protects the woodworker from electric shock.

Motor size
The size of electric motors for planers varies a great deal, but the average no-load speed is likely to be between 12,000 and 16,000rpm. Electronic systems provide gentle start-up and constant power under load.

Planing width
The cutters run the full width of the sole, which on the majority of planers is 3¼in (82mm).

Cutting depth
The sole of a planer is made in two sections, separated by the cylindrical cutter block. Raising the front or in-feed section increases the amount of wood the cutters can remove in one pass. Smaller planers have a maximum cutting depth of no more than ⅟₃₂in (1mm), whereas large professional-range machines will cut up to ⁵⁄₃₂in (3.5mm) deep. You can expect a good middle-range planer to remove up to ⅛in (2.5mm).

On most models, cutting depth is selected by adjusting a calibrated dial or knob mounted near the toe of the tool.

Rabbeting depth and width
An adjustable depth gauge mounted on the side of the machine determines the maximum depth of rabbet that can be cut with a planer. This will be between ¾ and 1in (20 and 24mm) with most planers, although some of the smaller tools may not be able to rabbet any deeper than ⁵⁄₁₆in (8mm). A side fence regulates the rabbet width. The normally square face of the fence can be adjusted to any angle up to 45 degrees for planing bevels accurately.

Chamfer-cutting groove
A V-groove machined down the center of the in-feed section of the sole positively locates the planer on a 90-degree corner for planing chamfers along a workpiece.

Cutter-block guard
A spring-loaded guard covers the cutter block completely until it is retracted automatically by the end of the workpiece as the planer is fed forward.

PLANER CUTTERS
A planer's cylindrical cutter block holds two balanced blades or cutters. There are straight general-purpose blades, which are usually tungsten-carbide tipped and often reversible. Straight cutters with rounded corners allow you to plane surfaces wider than the sole without leaving ridges in the wood. There are also wavy-edge cutters that simulate the tooled surface of "rustic" joinery.

Replace the cutters as soon as you feel you are having to apply too much force to the plane. Unplug the machine before you retract the cutter-block guard.

Straight cutter

Straight cutter with rounded corners

Wavy-edge cutter

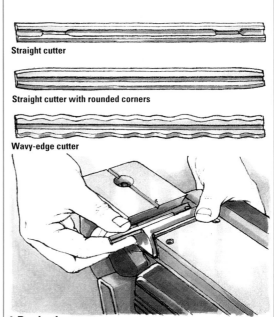

1 Replacing cutters
Your planer may have its own system for changing cutters, but the usual practice is to slide each blunt blade from a groove machined across the block and either reverse the blade or replace it with a new one.

2 Aligning cutters
Use a straight block of wood to align the end of each cutter with the edge of the sole, then tighten the clamping screws that secure the cutter in its groove.

POWER PLANING

As with any plane, it is always preferable to cut in the general direction of the grain; when planing rough grain, adjust the planer to take a finer cut. In any case, you will achieve a better finish if you plane down to the required depth in stages rather than try to remove the same amount of wood with a single pass. Check that there are no nails or screws in the work before you plane it; and don't be tempted to retract the guard except when changing cutters, having first unplugged the machine.

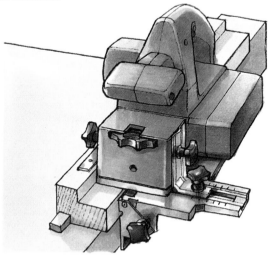

Handling a power planer
With the in-feed section of the sole resting on the work, switch on and advance the plane at a steady rate. Keep your weight on the toe of the tool until the entire sole is in contact with the wood. Near the end of each pass, transfer your weight to the rear of the planer to maintain a flat surface.

If possible, fit the side fence to help keep the planer square to the work; but if that is inconvenient, check the work with a try square after planing.

To plane a wide board flat, use the planer in the same manner as a bench plane (see page 51).

Planing a rabbet
To plane a rabbet along one edge of a workpiece, first set the side fence and depth gauge to the required dimensions. Proceed as described at left, keeping sideways pressure against the fence during each pass, until the depth gauge comes to rest on the top surface of the work.

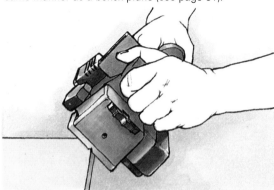

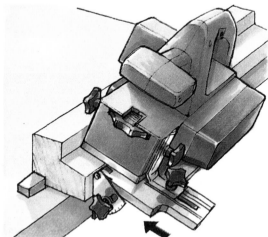

Planing a chamfer
Locate the V-groove in the in-feed sole on the square corner of the workpiece. Switch on and pass the plane from end to end, removing wood to the required depth in stages. Fit the angled side fence when planing a wide chamfer (see right).

Planing a beveled rabbet
In order to plane a beveled rabbet, adjust the face of the fence to tilt the whole plane at the required angle. It is absolutely vital to keep sideways pressure on the fence to prevent the planer from sliding down the slope.

BLOCK PLANES

The block plane is a lightweight tool primarily for trimming end grain. It is designed to be held in one hand, though pressure is applied to the toe of the plane with the other. Removing a metal lever cap reveals the blade, which is fitted bevel uppermost and used at a relatively shallow angle to the work surface to produce a paring action. Both wooden and metal block planes have comparatively sophisticated control over cutting depth and lateral movement of the blade, and the mouth of either plane can be adjusted to take fine shavings.

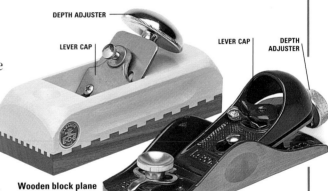

DEPTH ADJUSTER

LEVER CAP

LEVER CAP

DEPTH ADJUSTER

Wooden block plane

Metal block plane

Handling a block plane
Cup the bulbous lever cap or domed depth-adjusting knob in the palm of your hand, gripping the sides of the plane between fingers and thumb. While advancing the plane across the work, exert pressure on the toe with the thumb or fingertips of your free hand.

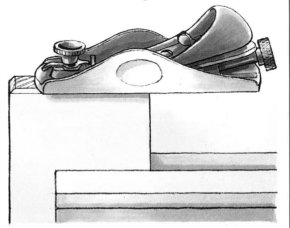

Preventing the wood from splitting
Alternatively, plane off one corner, down to the marked line, then plane the end grain towards the chamfered edge only.

Planing end grain
A razor-sharp blade is imperative when trimming end grain. Set the work upright in a bench vise, and plane from both sides towards the middle to prevent the wood from splitting from the edges.

Supporting the edge
Another method is to clamp a strip of waste wood flush with the end of the workpiece to support the edge and prevent it from splitting off.

RABBET AND SHOULDER PLANES

Various planes are made for cutting and trimming rabbets and other similar square-section recesses, such as dadoes and the shoulders of large joints. As they are somewhat specialized, you may not want to include all of them in your tool kit, but they can be invaluable when the needs arise.

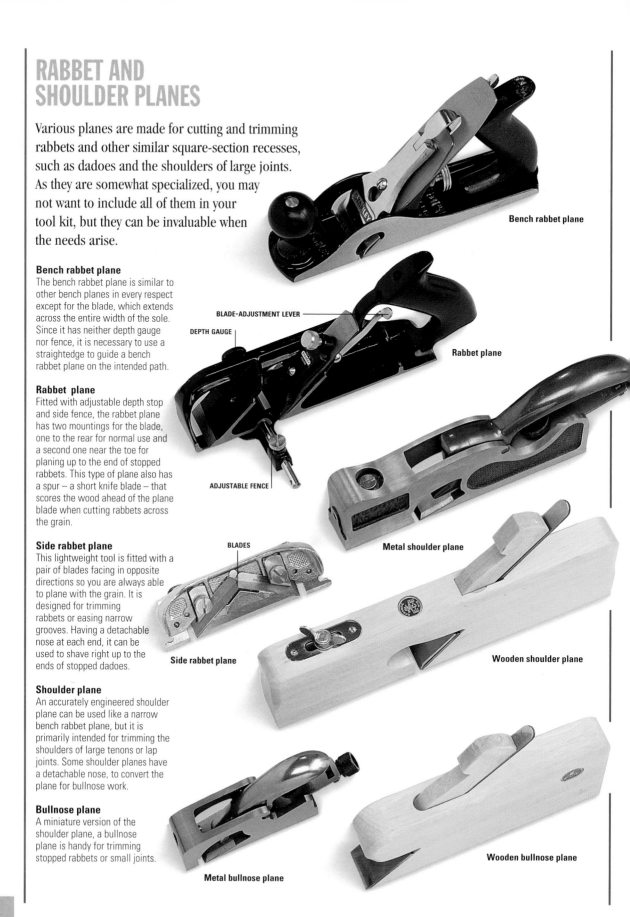

Bench rabbet plane

Bench rabbet plane
The bench rabbet plane is similar to other bench planes in every respect except for the blade, which extends across the entire width of the sole. Since it has neither depth gauge nor fence, it is necessary to use a straightedge to guide a bench rabbet plane on the intended path.

BLADE-ADJUSTMENT LEVER

DEPTH GAUGE

Rabbet plane

Rabbet plane
Fitted with adjustable depth stop and side fence, the rabbet plane has two mountings for the blade, one to the rear for normal use and a second one near the toe for planing up to the end of stopped rabbets. This type of plane also has a spur – a short knife blade – that scores the wood ahead of the plane blade when cutting rabbets across the grain.

ADJUSTABLE FENCE

Metal shoulder plane

Side rabbet plane
This lightweight tool is fitted with a pair of blades facing in opposite directions so you are always able to plane with the grain. It is designed for trimming rabbets or easing narrow grooves. Having a detachable nose at each end, it can be used to shave right up to the ends of stopped dadoes.

BLADES

Side rabbet plane

Wooden shoulder plane

Shoulder plane
An accurately engineered shoulder plane can be used like a narrow bench rabbet plane, but it is primarily intended for trimming the shoulders of large tenons or lap joints. Some shoulder planes have a detachable nose, to convert the plane for bullnose work.

Bullnose plane
A miniature version of the shoulder plane, a bullnose plane is handy for trimming stopped rabbets or small joints.

Metal bullnose plane

Wooden bullnose plane

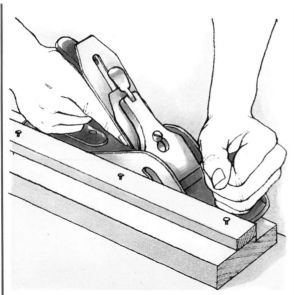

Guiding a bench rabbet plane

Score the depth of the intended rabbet on the edge of the workpiece and temporarily nail or clamp a straight batten to mark its inner edge. Holding the side of the plane hard up against the batten, start planing at the far end of the workpiece, gradually working backward as the rabbet begins to form. Take great care to keep the plane square to the work, and check regularly to ensure that you do not overrun the marked depth line.

Using a rabbet plane

Having set the depth gauge and fence, proceed as described at left, gradually increasing the length of stroke as the work progresses. Finally, plane the full length of the rabbet until the depth gauge prevents the blade from biting any deeper. To prevent cross-grain wood from splintering, lower the spur until its point can slice the fibers just ahead of the plane blade.

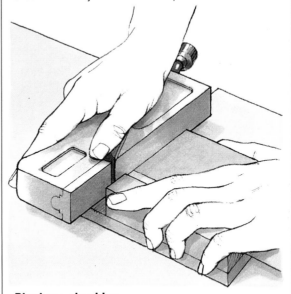

Using a side rabbet plane

Holding the plane on edge in the rabbet or groove, adjust the depth gauge on the back of the tool until it comes to rest on the top surface of the work. Run the plane against the vertical wall to trim the recess to size.

Planing a shoulder

Holding the work on a bench hook (see page 108), lay the plane on its side to pare the shoulder's end grain. Use a strip of scrap wood to prevent the wood from splitting along the back edge.

PLOW AND COMBINATION PLANES

The invention of a single tool that would combine the functions of dozens of wooden grooving, rabbeting and molding planes was in its day no less radical than the introduction of the power router, which was in turn destined to limit the appeal of these ingenious planes. Much loved by traditionalists, the simple plow plane, the more versatile combination plane and the multi-plane are all still available from specialist tool suppliers.

Plow plane
Supplied with a range of straight square-edged blades, the plow plane is designed specifically for cutting grooves or narrow dadoes. It comes complete with a depth gauge and side fence.

Combination plane
Similar in appearance to the plow plane, the combination plane includes a sliding clamp to hold the blade in place and a knurled screw to adjust the cutting depth. In addition to the usual depth gauge and side fence, the combination plane is equipped with a special narrow fence that facilitates the planing of a bead along a tongued edge – a feature that is often required for matchboarding. As well as standard blades, the combination plane can take a range of shaped cutters.

Multi-plane
A multi-plane is a combination plane with an even wider range of cutters, including a slitting knife for slicing strips of wood or moldings off a board. The kit includes a cam steady, a device that is fitted between the plane and side fence to prevent the fence supports from sagging when planing moldings some distance from the edge of a workpiece.

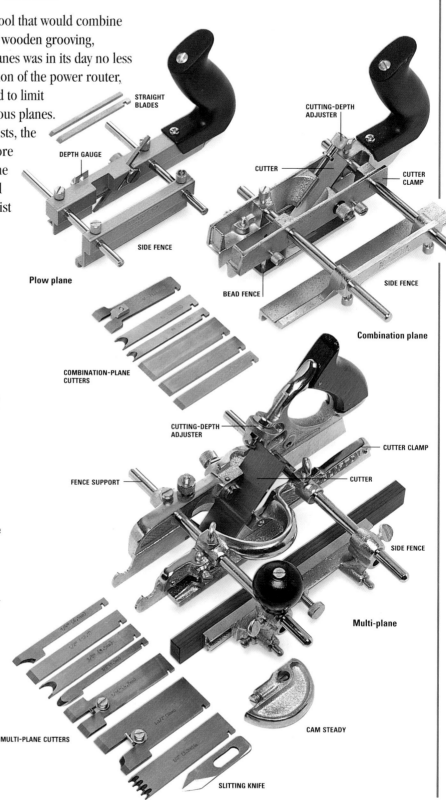

STRAIGHT BLADES

DEPTH GAUGE

SIDE FENCE

Plow plane

CUTTING-DEPTH ADJUSTER

CUTTER

CUTTER CLAMP

BEAD FENCE

SIDE FENCE

Combination plane

COMBINATION-PLANE CUTTERS

CUTTING-DEPTH ADJUSTER

CUTTER CLAMP

FENCE SUPPORT

CUTTER

SIDE FENCE

Multi-plane

MULTI-PLANE CUTTERS

CAM STEADY

SLITTING KNIFE

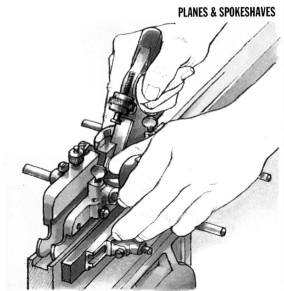

Handling the plane

Plow planes, combination planes and multi-planes are all held and controlled in a similar fashion. Keeping the side fence pressed against the work with your left hand, start to plane at the far end with short strokes, gradually working backwards until the plane is taking full-length shavings.

Cutting matching tongues and grooves

Set the depth stop on the cutter, and adjust the side fence to center the tongue on the edge of the workpiece. Plane the tongue as described above; then substitute a straight blade, and plane a matching but slightly deeper groove in the other workpiece.

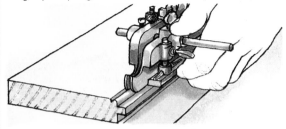

Cutting a bead along a tongued edge

Replace the standard side fence with the narrow bead fence, which runs against the edge of the work, just above the tongue. Set the depth gauge to ensure that the top of the bead remains almost flush with the surface of the work.

Plane cutters

The full range of cutters is shown above, together with the shape each one is designed to cut. From top to bottom, they are used as follows:

A *tongue cutter,* in combination with a matching straight cutter, makes a tongue-and-groove joint. The tongue cutter has its own adjustable depth stop.

A *sash-molding cutter* shapes one half of the window molding on the edge of a plank. The shape is repeated on the other side and the finished molding is cut from the plank, using the slitting knife.

An *ovolo cutter* is used to shape the edges of straight boards or all four sides of a panel.

A *bead cutter* is often used to disguise the joint between two boards.

A *reed cutter* produces a series of beads, side by side.

A *flute cutter* shapes hollows for finger pulls, pen holders and so on.

Straight cutters make rabbets and grooves.

SPOKESHAVES

A spokeshave is essentially a specialized plane for finishing curved workpieces and, once you get the hang of it, smoothing with a spokeshave is both fast and efficient. Every tool kit should contain at least straight-face and round-face versions of the standard spokeshave, whereas other less essential models can be acquired as and when required.

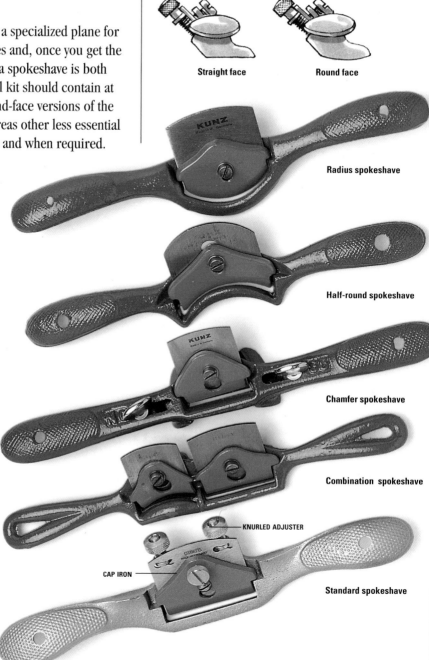

Straight face **Round face**

Radius spokeshave

Half-round spokeshave

Chamfer spokeshave

Combination spokeshave

KNURLED ADJUSTER

CAP IRON

Standard spokeshave

Standard spokeshave
A spokeshave is controlled by a straight handle mounted on each side of a short plane-like blade. The cutting depth and angle of the blade, which is held in place by a cast-metal cap iron, can be adjusted by means of two knurled screws. The blades in cheaper spokeshaves have no means of adjustment and are simply positioned by eye before the cap iron is inserted. Use a straight-face spokeshave to shape convex curves, and a round-face one to shave concave edges.

Radius spokeshave
This tool has a blade with a markedly convex cutting edge, making it ideal for finishing hollows such as those in solid-wood seats for traditional stick-back chairs.

Half-round spokeshave
This is a hollow-face spokeshave with a concave cutting edge. It is ideal for smoothing rounded edges of rails and legs.

Combination spokeshave
A dual-purpose spokeshave – with a standard blade mounted alongside a blade with a half-round cutting edge – saves having to swap one tool for another when working components with ever-changing profiles.

Chamfer spokeshave
This spokeshave is fitted with a pair of adjustable fences that allow for cutting accurate chamfers along a workpiece with 90-degree corners.

Controlling a spokeshave
To cut smoothly, it is essential to have precise control over the angle of the blade. This is achieved by taking hold of the tool with your thumbs resting on the back edges of the handles. With the face of the spokeshave resting on the work, push it forward, rocking the tool back and forth until you begin to take a shaving cleanly. Shave a curve in two directions, to ensure you are always cutting with the grain.

CHAPTER 5 The router has probably made more impact on woodworking than any other power tool, at least since the introduction of the electric drill. It is a remarkably versatile machine, so much so that one can only hope to cover the basic operations in a few pages. More advanced procedures, such as longitudinal fluting or beading and cutting woodworking joints with the aid of specialized jigs, fall outside the scope of this book.

POWER ROUTERS

POWER ROUTERS

You can set up a power router in about the same time it takes to adjust a handtool to do a similar job and, because the router cutter is driven at relatively high speeds, the results are invariably precise and professional in appearance.

Most modern routers are fundamentally similar: a precision-ground cutter is fitted into the bottom of a motor housing that has a handgrip mounted on each side. The housing rides up and down on a pair of metal columns attached to the tool's base plate. Pressing down on the handgrips plunges the cutter through a hole in the base plate and into the wood; strong coil springs raise the housing automatically as soon as you release the pressure on the handgrips. There are also fixed-based routers that do not plunge.

Base plate
The base plate carries all the clamps that secure the various accessories, including the side fence and dust-extraction hood. A replaceable plastic facing prevents the metal base plate from marking the wood.

Depth stop
The depth stop determines how far a cutter projects from the base of the router, and therefore how deeply it can cut into the wood. Because it is good practice to make deep cuts in stages, most routers incorporate a turret stop which enables you to pre-set up to three different cutting depths.

Spindle lock
On most modern routers, the spindle is immobilized by pressing a button, enabling you to turn the collet nut with a wrench when changing a cutter.

Plunge lock
A mechanism enables you to lock the cutter at any height. In the model shown, the lock is built into one of the handgrips.

Side fence
An adjustable side fence, which guides the cutter on a path parallel to the straight edge of a workpiece, is virtually standard equipment and is often supplied with the router as part of the kit.

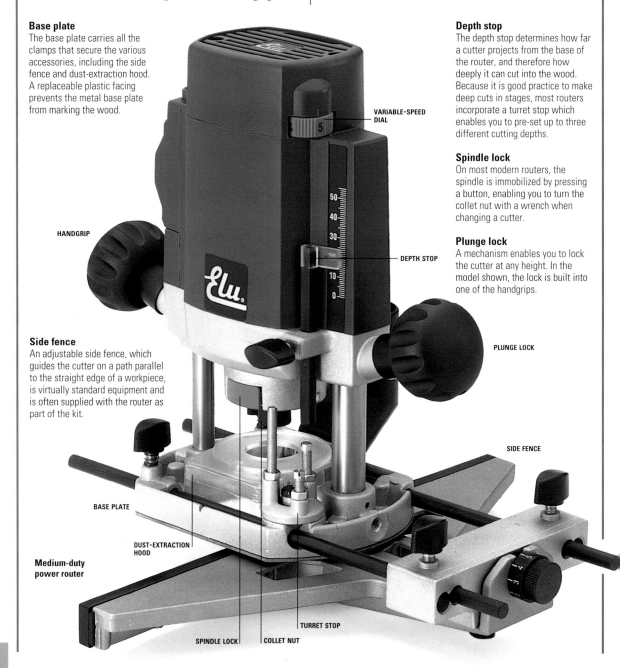

HANDGRIP

VARIABLE-SPEED DIAL

DEPTH STOP

PLUNGE LOCK

SIDE FENCE

BASE PLATE

DUST-EXTRACTION HOOD

Medium-duty power router

SPINDLE LOCK

COLLET NUT

TURRET STOP

Size of router

A medium-duty router of around 1¼ to 1¾HP (800 to 1200W) is perhaps ideal for the amateur workshop. You will find that most factory-made accessories, jigs and templates are made for this category of router, which is more than adequate for making furniture and light joinery. There are less expensive, light-duty routers, fitted with motors of up to 1HP (750W), which can cope with most basic operations, including grooving, rabbeting and molding. However, a more powerful machine will probably complete the same tasks in less time, and you may find that the choice of cutters for light-duty routers is limited. A professional would probably opt for a heavy-duty router with a motor of up to 2½HP (1850W), which is capable of driving the large-diameter cutters required for building construction.

Collet capacity

The shank of a router cutter fits into a tapered collet mounted directly below the electric motor. Tightening the collet nut locks the cutter in place. Most router collets are designed to accommodate ¼ or ⅜in (6 or 8mm) diameter shanks, but larger routers have a collet capacity of ½in (12mm).

Variable speed control

The majority of routers are available with variable speed control, so that you can select the optimum spindle speed for the job in hand. For most operations, you can operate a router at maximum speed (20,000 to 30,000rpm, depending on the tool's power output) – but you would need to reduce the speed when using a large-diameter cutter, for example. Similarly, relatively low spindle speeds are required when machining soft metals and plastics, and also to reduce the risk of scorching wood when making intricate freehand cuts. Router manufacturers supply recommended operating speeds for particular models.

Electronic monitoring maintains a constant speed, even when the feed rate changes or you encounter a tough section of timber. It also eliminates the familiar "kick" on starting up. Spindle speed is usually selected by turning a dial before switching on the router.

Dust extraction

Dust-extraction facilities are available for all power routers. On some models the extraction unit comes as a permanent fixture, but in most cases it takes the form of a transparent plastic hood that encloses the cutter. The hood is connected to a flexible hose that diverts the waste to an industrial vacuum cleaner. For clarity, the dust-extraction hood and hose have been omitted from most of the illustrations in this book.

Guide bushings

Most routers can be fitted with guide bushings for use with jigs and templates (see page 68).

ROUTER PLANES

Although this chapter is concerned almost exclusively with power routers, it is impossible to exclude the router plane which was once almost exclusively used for cutting dadoes across a board or panel. To do so, first saw down both sides of the dado; then use the router plane, fitted with an L-shape cutter, to remove the waste in stages, adjusting the depth of cut each time the base of the dado has been leveled.

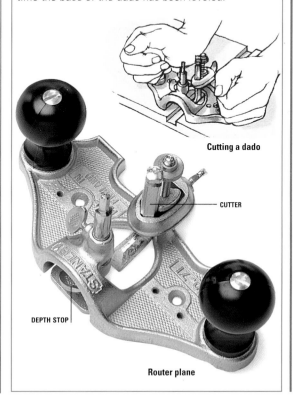

Cutting a dado

CUTTER

DEPTH STOP

Router plane

ROUTER CUTTERS

Router cutters are expensive – especially those with large or complex profiles – and, since no woodworker needs to acquire the full range available, it makes sense to buy them as the need arises, spending as much as you can afford at the time in order to get only good-quality cutters.

High-speed-steel (HSS) cutters are perfectly adequate for most woodworking applications, but you will find that the more expensive tungsten-carbide-tipped (TCT) cutters are a better buy in the long run because they hold their edge longer, especially when routing tough hardwoods and abrasive man-made boards. When plunge-cutting, choose a cutter with cutting edges that extend across its tip; a cutter made without bottom-cutting edges can only be fed into the work from the side.

Plain or fence-guided cutters
This type of cutter has to be guided on its intended path by means of the adjustable side fence or a trammel, or by running the router's base plate against a straightedge. Plain cutters are also used when routing freehand or with a guide bushing and template.

Self-guiding cutters
This type of cutter is manufactured with a solid pin ground on its tip or with a ball-bearing guide mounted on the tip or the shank, just above the cutting edges. With their pilot tips or bearings running against the edge of a workpiece or template, self-guiding cutters can be used to machine a variety of edge moldings and rabbets. Self-guiding cutters are also made for trimming veneers and plastic laminates flush with a workpiece.

CHANGING ROUTER CUTTERS
To remove a cutter, unplug the router, depress the spindle lock and loosen the collet nut with a wrench. When inserting another cutter, ensure that at least three-quarters of the shank is held in the collet.

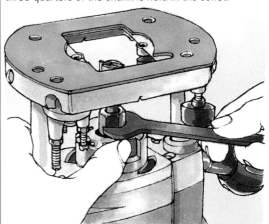

Turn a router upside down to prevent the cutter from dropping onto the bench when you loosen the collet nut

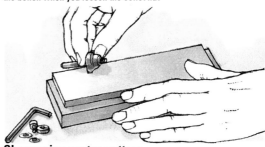

Sharpening router cutters
To sharpen an HSS cutter, hone the flat faces of the cutting edges on an oilstone. Never attempt to hone the beveled edges. Remove the bearing race before sharpening a self-guiding cutter; or if the pin is integral, take care not to run it against the stone. It may pay to have TCT cutters reground professionally, but it is possible to hone them yourself on a diamond-impregnated stone.

Groove cutters

The following selection of plain or fence-guided router cutters can machine recesses both parallel with or across the grain.

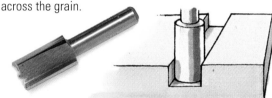

Straight cutters

The basic router cutter machines square-section grooves or dadoes. Most straight cutters are manufactured with either one or two cutting edges. The latter (known as two-flute cutters) leave a better finish, but a single-flute cutter clears waste more efficiently.

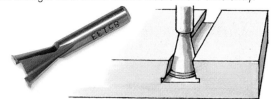

Dovetail cutters

Designed primarily for machining dovetail joints, these cutters are also useful for making dovetail dadoes.

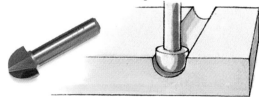

Radius or core-box cutters

These cutters can be used to machine single round-bottomed grooves or a series of parallel flutes.

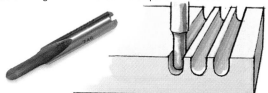

Veining cutters

Create narrow and relatively deep round-bottomed grooves with a veining cutter.

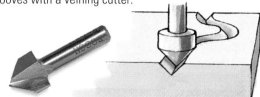

V-groove cutters

These are used primarily for decorative low-relief carving and freehand lettering.

Edge-forming cutters

Groove cutters can be used in conjunction with a guide fence to machine the edges of a workpiece, but the majority of edge-forming cutters are made with a self-guiding tip or bearing (see opposite).

Rabbet cutters

Depth of cut is determined by how far the cutter projects from the router base. Some cutters can be fitted with different-size bearings to alter the rabbet width.

Chamfer cutters

Used to machine 45-degree bevels along the edges of the work. The same cutter can be employed to cut different-size chamfers simply by adjusting the router's depth stop.

Round-over cutters

These cutters produce a simple rounded edge or, when set lower, a stepped ovolo bead.

Cove cutters

You can produce decorative scalloped edges with a cove cutter or, in combination with a similar round-over cutter, machine a rule joint for a drop-leaf table.

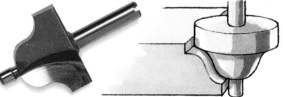

Decorative-molding cutters

There are a great many cutters designed to produce molded edges on frames or panels.

CUTTING GROOVES AND DADOES

Cutting a groove accurately is essential when fitting drawer bottoms and when fixing the back panel into a cupboard. A true groove runs parallel with the grain; when a groove is cut across the grain, it is known as a dado. Dadoes are used a great deal for fixed shelving and for attaching drawer runners on the inside of a cabinet. Used with a side fence or a straightedge guide, the power router is the ideal tool for machining both grooves and dadoes.

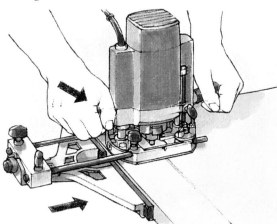

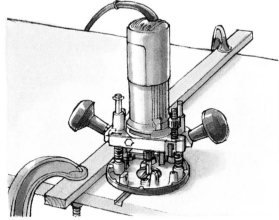

Grooving with a side fence

When machining a groove relatively close to the edge of a panel, first place the router on the surface, aligning the cutter with a pencil mark drawn across the workpiece. Slide the fence up against the edge of the work and tighten the fence clamps.

To cut a through groove, plunge and lock the cutter, then rest the front half of the base plate on the work with the cutter clear of the edge. Switch on and feed the cutter into the work, keeping the fence held firmly against the guide edge. Continue with the pass until the cutter emerges from the opposite edge of the work, then switch off before releasing the plunge lock.

Clearly mark the ends of a stopped groove with a pencil and position the router as described above. Switch on and plunge the cutter into the work, then feed it forward at a steady rate until you reach the other end of the groove. Back off slightly before lifting the cutter clear and switching off.

Grooving an edge

Fit a second side fence to prevent a router from rocking when machining a narrow workpiece. Set the distance between the fences to leave minimal side play, but before switching on, check that you can feed the router smoothly.

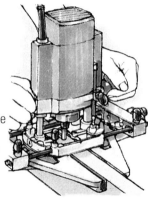

Cutting a dado

When a dado is too far from the edge of a workpiece to use a side fence, clamp a straight batten across the work to guide the edge of the base plate. Although most dadoes are square to the edges of the workpiece, you can clamp a batten at any angle.

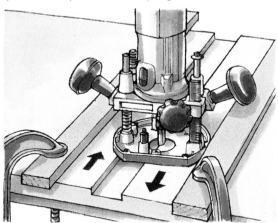

Cutting a wide dado

To machine a dado that is wider than the router cutter, use a pair of parallel guide battens to align a cutting edge with each side of the dado. Machine one side of the dado, then move the router across to the other batten to make a second pass in the opposite direction. Make each pass against the rotation of the cutter; this helps to keep the base plate pressed against the guide battens.

CUTTING RABBETS AND EDGE MOLDINGS

Cutting a rabbet and molding the edge of a workpiece with a router require a similar procedure. Feed the router against the direction of cutter rotation, so that the rotational force tends to pull the cutter into the work.

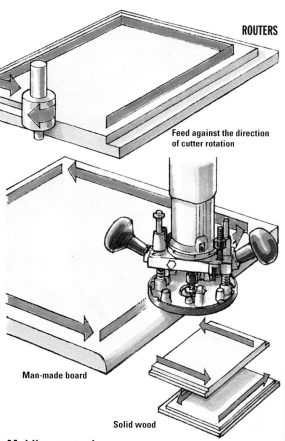

Feed against the direction of cutter rotation

Man-made board

Solid wood

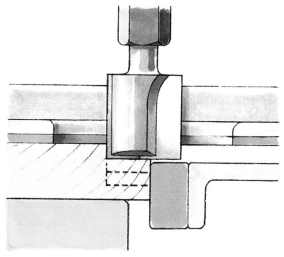

Rabbeting with a fence
Fit a straight router cutter with a diameter that is larger than the width of the rabbet. Adjust the side fence to align the cutting edge with the inner face of the rabbet. Cut in a series of shallow steps, until you reach the required depth.

Molding a panel
Mold all four sides of a panel as described below left, feeding the router counterclockwise. However, if the panel is made from solid wood, machine the end grain first; any split edges will be removed when you mold the side grain.

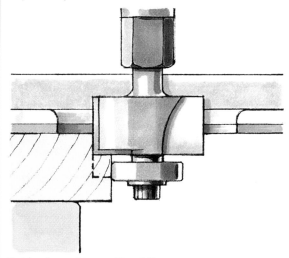

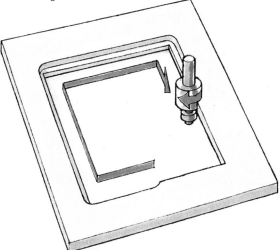

Rabbeting with a self-guiding cutter
Self-guiding rabbet cutters can be used on straight or curved edges. Run the bearing tip against the edge of the work, adjusting the cutting depth between passes until the rabbet is complete.

Molding inside a frame
When you are molding or rabbeting the inside of a frame, feed the router clockwise. Router cutters leave rabbets with rounded corners, but you can trim them square with a wood chisel.

CUTTING CIRCLES AND SHAPED WORKPIECES

Special attachments are available to help you cut perfect disks or holes with a power router, and to replicate intricately shaped workpieces.

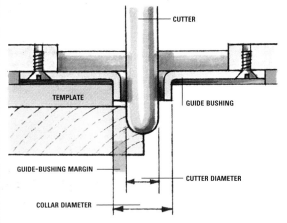

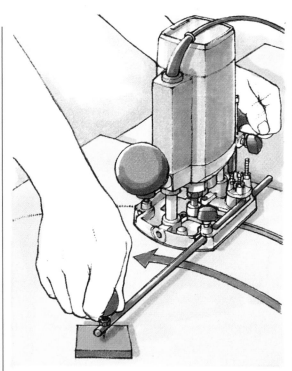

Guide-bushing margin

A metal guide bushing (see page 63) enables you to follow a homemade template with a router – a quick and easy method for making any number of identical pieces. A guide bushing, bolted to the base plate, is essentially a circular collar that surrounds the cutter. The collar runs against the edge of the template, and the cutter faithfully reproduces its profile. When designing and making a template, you need to allow for the guide-bushing margin – the difference between the diameter of the collar and the diameter of the cutter itself.

Using a trammel

A trammel – a rigid metal rod or bar with a pin at one end – is used to rotate a router about a center point for cutting arcs or circles. A trammel rod attaches to the side-fence clamps. To prevent the trammel-pin from marking the work, use double-sided adhesive tape to stick a small plywood patch over the center point.

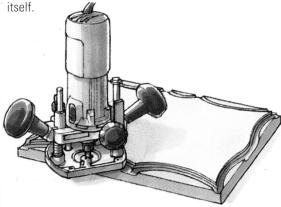

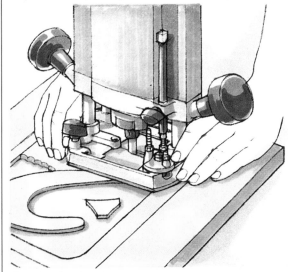

Routing with a template

Cut a template from a smooth, stable sheet material such as MDF. The template must be thick enough to keep the guide bushing clear of the work, but not so thick that you cannot achieve the required depth of cut. Pin the template to the work, or hold it in place with double-sided adhesive tape.

Routing freehand

Provided your hand-and-eye coordination is up to the task, you can rout any shape you like without having to use templates or guides of any sort. Adjust the router to take a very shallow cut and, holding the base plate with your hands lightly in contact with the work, use a free-flowing action to control the router and keep it moving.

CHAPTER *6*   A set of chisels and a selection of basic gouges are essential tools for every workshop. They are used primarily for removing the waste from joints and for shaping and trimming workpieces. Provided your chisels and gouges are kept sharp, you can drive them through the wood using hand pressure only, but sometimes it is more convenient to use a carpenter's mallet, especially when there's a lot of waste to be removed.

CHISELS & GOUGES

CHISELS

Firmer and bevel-edge chisels are made with blades that range from about ¼ to 1½in (6 to 38mm) wide, but basic sets of chisels offered for sale hardly ever include one that is wider than 1in (25mm).

Firmer chisel
The firmer chisel, with its relatively thick rectangular-section blade, is the woodworker's general-purpose chisel. It is strong enough to be driven with a mallet through the toughest hardwood.

Bevel-edge chisel
This is a comparatively lightweight chisel, designed for trimming and shaping workpieces by hand. The blade is flat on the underside, like a firmer chisel, but shallow bevels are ground along both long edges on the upper face so that you can trim dovetailed undercuts.

Paring chisel
This is a specialized bevel-edge chisel with an extra-long blade for removing waste from dado joints. A chisel with a cranked neck allows you to keep the blade flat on the work even when paring wood from the center of a wide panel or board.

Skew chisel
The end of the blade is ground to an angle of 60 degrees to produce a slicing action as the chisel is driven forward. This makes for smooth cutting, even through rough grain or knotty timber.

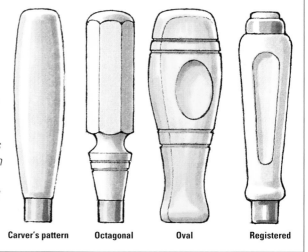

Firmer chisel

Bevel-edge chisel

Paring chisel

Cranked paring chisel

Skew chisel

CHISEL HANDLES

A great many chisels are still made with tough hardwood handles, but there is a popular trend for molded plastic handles that are practically indestructible even when driven with a metal hammer, a practice that would ruin a wooden handle. Traditional cylindrical carver's-pattern handles provide a comfortable ergonomic grip. An octagonal handle prevents a chisel from rolling off the bench, as does the more common oval grip, usually molded from plastic. A registered handle is reinforced at the butt end with a metal hoop to prevent the wood's splitting under constant hammering from a mallet.

Carver's pattern   **Octagonal**   **Oval**   **Registered**

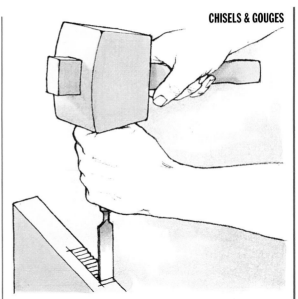

Paring with a chisel

Clamp the work to a bench or steady it against a bench hook. Grip the chisel handle in one hand, with your index finger extended towards the blade. Keep your forearm in line with the chisel and tuck your elbow into your side. With your free hand, grip the blade behind the cutting edge between index finger and thumb. As you apply pressure to the handle, use the other hand to guide the blade and control the force applied to the cutting edge.

Driving a chisel with a mallet

To drive a chisel through tough hardwood or chop the waste from deep joints, place the cutting edge on the work, then strike the butt end of the handle with a carpenter's mallet. For more delicate work, such as removing the waste from a hinge recess, grip the mallet shaft just below the head and tap the handle, using just the weight of the mallet to do the work.

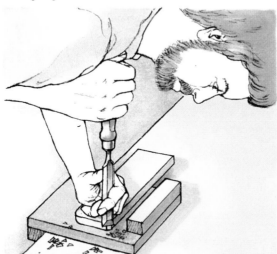

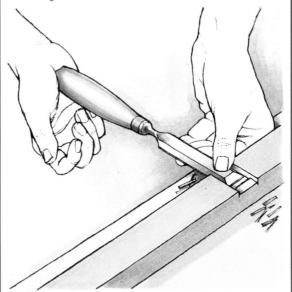

Trimming end grain

To shape the end of a workpiece, place the wood flat on a bench hook or a piece of scrap board. Hold the chisel upright, with your thumb curled over the butt end of the handle. Rest your free hand on the work, controlling the blade by allowing it to slide between your index finger and thumb. Apply firm, steady pressure to the chisel with your shoulder.

Using hand pressure

If you need to apply extra force when paring wood from a recess, either tap the chisel with a mallet or, keeping your forearm in line with the blade, strike the end of the handle with the ball of your hand.

MORTISE CHISELS

Cutting deep mortises requires a chisel which will not jam in the work and which is strong enough to be used as a lever to remove the waste. Many mortise chisels are fitted with leather shock-absorbing washers between the handle and the blade.

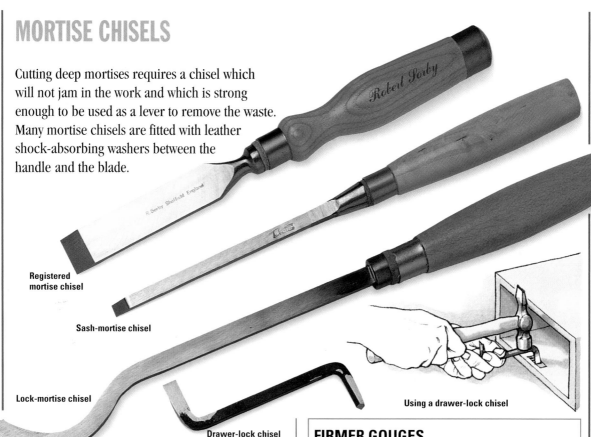

Registered mortise chisel

Sash-mortise chisel

Lock-mortise chisel

Drawer-lock chisel

Using a drawer-lock chisel

Registered mortise chisel
This type of chisel is similar in appearance to an ordinary firmer chisel, but the blade tapers in thickness towards the cutting edge so that it will not become jammed in a deep mortise. Registered mortise chisels are available in widths up to 2in (50mm).

Sash-mortise chisel
To cut deep but narrow mortises, choose a sash-mortise chisel with a thick tapered blade up to ½in (12mm) wide.

Lock-mortise chisel
A swan-neck lock-mortise chisel is used to level the bottom of a deep mortise cut with a sash-mortise chisel. Use one that is the same size or slightly smaller than the chisel used to cut the mortise.

Drawer-lock chisel
An all-metal, cranked drawer-lock chisel is designed for working in confined spaces where it would be impossible to wield an ordinary chisel and mallet. It has two cutting edges, one parallel to the shaft and the other at right angles to it. Strike the cranked shaft with a hammer, just above one of the cutting edges.

FIRMER GOUGES
A gouge is a chisel with a blade that is curved in cross section. An out-cannel gouge – with the cutting edge ground on the back of the blade – is used to scoop out hollows. An in-cannel gouge has the cutting edge ground on the top face of the blade and can be used to trim curved shoulders, such as for a chair rail that is to be joined to turned legs. Gouges range from ¼ to 1in (6 to 25mm) in width.

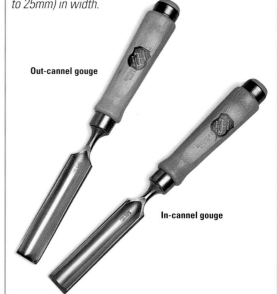

Out-cannel gouge

In-cannel gouge

CHAPTER 7 The availability of power drills, especially the range of improved cordless tools, has greatly reduced the need for hand-operated drills and ratchet braces. However, despite their versatility, electric drills have not completely eradicated the demand for handtools which are comparatively inexpensive, quiet and perfectly safe in the hands of young or inexperienced woodworkers.

HAND DRILLS AND BRACES

Rugged but lightweight hand drills and ratchet braces are convenient for working "on site," since they are completely independent of any power source. A brace is especially useful for boring holes up to 2in (50mm) in diameter and can also be used to drive large woodscrews.

1 Dowel bits
2 Countersink bit
3 Twist drills
4 Jennings-pattern bit
5 Solid-center auger bit
6 Expansive bits
7 Center bit
8 Screwdriver bit
9 Brace countersink bit

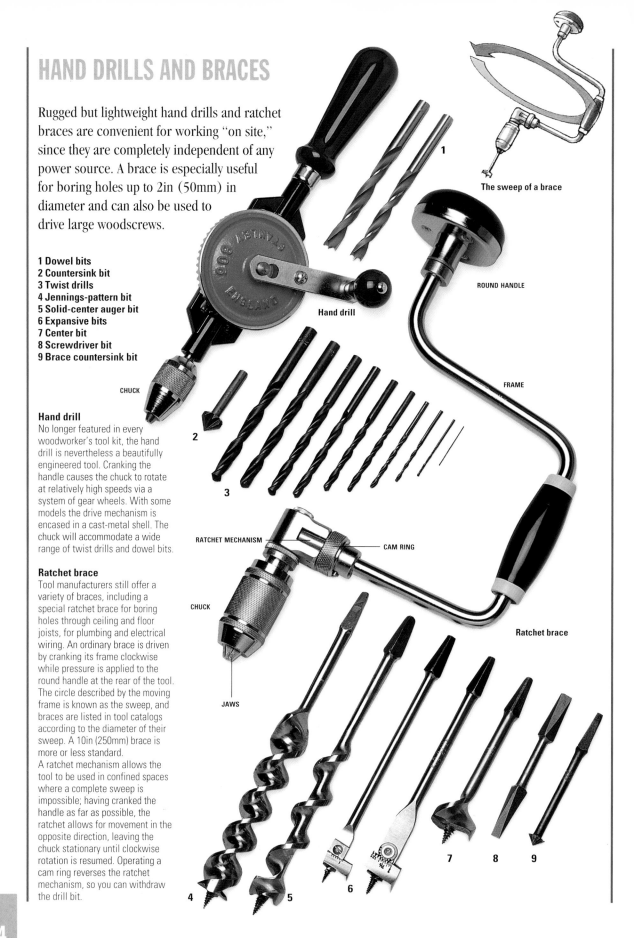

The sweep of a brace

ROUND HANDLE

FRAME

Hand drill

CHUCK

RATCHET MECHANISM

CAM RING

CHUCK

JAWS

Ratchet brace

Hand drill
No longer featured in every woodworker's tool kit, the hand drill is nevertheless a beautifully engineered tool. Cranking the handle causes the chuck to rotate at relatively high speeds via a system of gear wheels. With some models the drive mechanism is encased in a cast-metal shell. The chuck will accommodate a wide range of twist drills and dowel bits.

Ratchet brace
Tool manufacturers still offer a variety of braces, including a special ratchet brace for boring holes through ceiling and floor joists, for plumbing and electrical wiring. An ordinary brace is driven by cranking its frame clockwise while pressure is applied to the round handle at the rear of the tool. The circle described by the moving frame is known as the sweep, and braces are listed in tool catalogs according to the diameter of their sweep. A 10in (250mm) brace is more or less standard.
A ratchet mechanism allows the tool to be used in confined spaces where a complete sweep is impossible; having cranked the handle as far as possible, the ratchet allows for movement in the opposite direction, leaving the chuck stationary until clockwise rotation is resumed. Operating a cam ring reverses the ratchet mechanism, so you can withdraw the drill bit.

Drill bits

The jaws of a hand drill take cylindrical twist drills and dowel bits. Braces are designed to accommodate special square-shanked bits, but some have universal jaws which will also accept cylindrical-shank drills.

Twist drills

Simple twist drills are made with a pair of helical flutes (twisted grooves) that clear the waste from the hole as the drill bores into the wood. The flutes culminate in two cutting edges that form a pointed tip to the drill. Most hand drills take bits up to a maximum diameter of ⅜in (9mm). Many woodworkers opt for a set of twist drills that will bore into metal as well as wood.

Dowel bits

These are wood-boring twist drills with sharp lead points that prevent them from wandering off line. Two sharp spurs per bit cut a clean-edged hole.

Auger bits

A solid-center auger bit for a ratchet brace has a single helical twist that brings the waste to the surface and serves to keep the bit on line when boring deep holes. It has a pair of spurs at the cutting tip that score the wood ahead of the cutting edges to ensure a crisp edge to the hole. The lead screw in the center pulls the bit into the wood. The similar Jennings-pattern auger bit has a double helical twist. Auger bits range from ¼ to 1½in (6 to 38mm) in diameter.

Expansive bits

An adjustable expansive bit will cut a hole of any size between limits. Depending on the model, an expansive bit is capable of cutting holes between ½ and 1½in (12 and 38mm) in diameter or, alternatively, between ⅞ and 3in (22 and 75mm).

Center bits

Since center bits are designed to bore relatively shallow holes, from 2¾ to 4½in (68 to 112mm) deep, they are simpler and therefore cheaper than the equivalent auger bits.

Screwdriver bits

A special double-ended bit converts a brace into a heavy-duty screwdriver.

Countersink bits

Countersink bits, whether for a hand drill or a brace, are used to cut tapered recesses in order to accommodate the heads of woodscrews so they lie flush with the surface of the work.

Operating a hand-drill chuck

To open the jaws of a hand drill, hold the chuck in one hand and crank the handle counterclockwise. Load a drill bit, then grip the chuck and turn the handle clockwise to tighten the jaws.

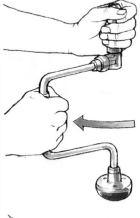

Fitting a bit into a ratchet brace

Lock the brace ratchet by centering the cam ring, then grip the chuck in one hand and turn the frame clockwise. Drop a bit into the chuck and reverse the action to close the jaws.

Using a hand drill

Place the tip of the drill bit on the work and gently move the handle back and forth until the bit begins to bite into the wood. Crank the handle at speed to bore a hole to the required depth. Don't apply too much pressure when using small twist drills; the weight of the tool alone will be sufficient to encourage the drill to penetrate the wood.

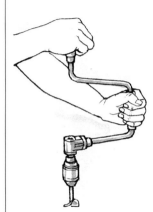

Boring with a brace

Hold the brace upright with one hand while cranking the frame with the other. To bore horizontally, steady the round handle against your body. To retrieve the bit, lock the ratchet and reverse the action a couple of turns to release the lead screw; then pull on the tool while moving the frame back and forth.

POWER DRILLS

A power drill is not only an invaluable woodworking tool – most people also own at least one corded or cordless drill for household repairs and maintenance. Consequently there is an immense range of drills on the market, from cheap, virtually "throwaway" tools to durable and sophisticated drills for the professional carpenter and woodworker. Although a middle-of-the-range drill is adequate for woodworking, it makes sense to choose a tool that will satisfy all possible requirements.

Corded electric drills
Most woodworkers continue to opt for corded electric drills. They may be relatively heavy and bulky, but they are extremely tough and reliable tools that will run more or less continuously for hours on end, provided you have access to a power supply.

Hammer action
Throwing a switch engages the drill's hammer action which delivers several hundred blows per second behind the drill bit to help break up masonry when boring into stone or brick walls. Hammer action is never required for woodwork.

SPEED SELECTION

HAMMER-ACTION SWITCH

DEPTH STOP

KEYLESS CHUCK

BOSCH

CSB 550 RP

550 W · Beton Ø max. 15 mm

Corded electric drill

REVERSE-ACTION SWITCH

VARIABLE-SPEED TRIGGER

LOCK BUTTON

Drill chucks
Most chucks have three self-centering jaws that grip the shank of a drill bit. Some chucks need tightening with a special toothed key to ensure that the drill bit is held securely by the jaws and will not slip in use, but a great many drills are made with "keyless" chucks, which take a firm grip on the bit simply by turning a cylindrical collar that surrounds the mechanism.

Depth stop
An adjustable depth stop comes to rest against the work when the drill bit has bored to the required depth.

Reverse action
A reverse-action switch changes the direction of rotation so that the power drill can be used to extract woodscrews.

Trigger lock
Depressing a button on the drill's handle locks the trigger for continuous running. Squeezing the trigger again releases the lock button.

Speed selection
Although a few basic drills have a limited range of fixed speeds selected by operating a switch, the majority of drills are variable-speed tools, controlled by the amount of pressure applied to the trigger. On some models, it is also possible to select the maximum rotational speed by turning a small dial that limits the movement of the trigger. Many drills also incorporate electronic speed-control systems that maintain optimum speed when the load applied to the drill bit changes. A similar system will often protect the motor from damage if the bit jams in the work and may also minimize the initial jolt as the high-speed electric motor starts up. Manufacturers recommend a range of speeds at which their drills will perform best; however, as a rule of thumb, select a fast speed for boring into wood, but slower speeds for drilling metal and masonry and to drive woodscrews.

1

2

3

4

1 Countersink bit
2 Drill-and-countersink bit
3 Drill-and-counterbore bit
4 Plug cutter

Power-drill bits

Most power drills have a chuck capacity – the maximum size of drill-bit shank that the chuck will accommodate – of ⅜ or ½in (10 or 13mm). The shank size of a twist drill or dowel bit (see page 75) corresponds exactly to the size of hole that a particular bit will bore. However, a great many wood-boring bits are capable of making holes larger than their shank diameter.

Reduced-shank twist drills

Twist drills ½ to 1in (13 to 25mm) in diameter are made with reduced shanks that will fit a standard-size power-drill chuck. Twist drills are not easy to locate on the dead center of a hole; when drilling hardwoods, in particular, it therefore pays to mark the center of a hole first, using a metalworking punch.

Spade bits

These are inexpensive drill bits made for power-drilling large holes from ¼ to 1½in (6 to 38mm) in diameter. A long lead point makes for positive location even when drilling at an angle to the face of the work.

Forstner bits

Forstner bits leave exceptionally clean flat-bottomed holes up to 2in (50mm) in diameter. Because the bit will not be deflected, even by rough grain or knots, you can bore overlapping holes and holes that run out to the edge of the work without difficulty.

Countersink bits

Similar to the countersink bits made for hand drills and braces (see page 75), these drill bits are used to make tapered recesses for the heads of woodscrews. Center the bit on a clearance hole bored in the wood, and run the power drill at a high speed for a clean finish.

Drill-and-countersink bits

These specialized drill bits cut a pilot hole, clearance hole and countersink for a woodscrew in one operation. Each bit is matched to a particular size of screw.

Drill-and-counterbore bits

Instead of cutting a tapered recess for a screw head, this type of bit leaves a neat hole that allows the screw to be driven below the face of the workpiece.

Plug cutters

These cut cylindrical plugs of wood to hide the heads of counterbored woodscrews.

Screwdriver bits

These are made to drive slotted and cross-head screws.

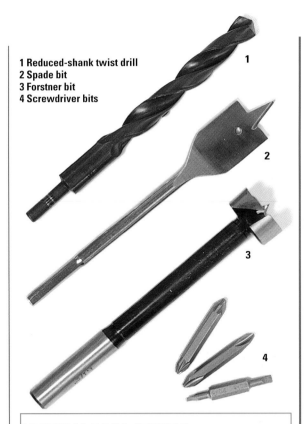

1 Reduced-shank twist drill
2 Spade bit
3 Forstner bit
4 Screwdriver bits

VERTICAL DRILL STANDS

A vertical stand converts a portable power drill into a serviceable drill press. Pulling on the spring-loaded feed lever lowers the drill bit into the wood; the depth of stopped holes can be pre-set, using a gauge on the stand. Bolt or screw the cast-metal base to a bench.

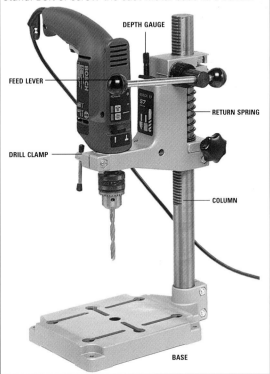

DEPTH GAUGE
FEED LEVER
RETURN SPRING
DRILL CLAMP
COLUMN
BASE

CORDLESS DRILLS

Battery-powered drills have certain advantages over those that have cords, the most obvious being their portability and independence of a power supply. There's no cord to get caught on obstructions, and very little noise when running.

Although there are cordless drills with a chuck capacity of ½in (13mm), most models have ⅜in (10mm) chucks; but even the latter can bore holes up to 1¼in (30mm), using reduced-shank bits (see page 77).

KEYLESS CHUCK

TORQUE SELECTION

BLACK&DECKER®
VP7251C

REVERSE-ACTION SWITCH
AND SAFETY LOCK

VARIABLE-SPEED TRIGGER

VERSAPAK™

SCREWDRIVER BIT

PRESS   PRESS

RECHARGEABLE BATTERY

Battery-operated power drill

Charging cordless drills
Some drills are supplied with a wall-hung charging unit: when the drill is returned to the unit after use, it is recharged automatically. However, most cordless drills have removable battery packs that are inserted into a separate plug-in charger; having a spare battery pack on charge means you will never be left without power.

It can take anything from one to three hours to fully recharge a battery, but you can buy rapid chargers that will do the job in 15 minutes or less. Most battery packs can be recharged several thousand times before they need replacing.

Driving screws with a cordless drill
Variable-speed drills with electronic control are ideal for driving woodscrews. Before screwing into hardwoods, first drill a pilot hole and a clearance hole for the screw shank. Countersink the hole if required.

Locate the screwdriver bit in the screw slot before switching on, and maintain pressure on the drill the whole time to prevent the bit from slipping. You will find that a cross-head tip makes for more positive location. All cordless drills have reverse-action for removing screws: one with a torque setting allows you to drive a screw flush without overiding and damaging the screw slot.

Chapter 8 Although nails are rarely used for fine woodworking, they are often employed when constructing mock-ups and for carpentry. Consequently, most tool kits boast a range of hammers of different weights. Wooden mallets and so-called soft hammers are also required for driving wood chisels and gouges, and for assembling or dismantling joints.

HAMMERS

A surprising number of accidents are caused by hammer heads working loose or by poor-quality shafts breaking in use. It is never worth economizing by buying cheap hammers since even the best-quality tools are relatively inexpensive.

Cross-peen hammer
A medium-weight, 10 to 12oz (280 to 340g), cross-peen hammer is adequate as a general-purpose woodworking hammer. The cross peen – the wedge opposite the striking face – is used to start small nails held between finger and thumb. As with most good hammers, the top end of the ash or hickory shaft is preshrunk and sealed in oil before being driven into the hammer head and expanded with hornbeam and iron wedges to lock the head securely to the shaft.

Pin hammer
The pin hammer is a lightweight cross-peen hammer for driving small nails, panel pins and tacks.

Claw hammer
Most carpenters choose a 20 or 24oz (570 or 680g) claw hammer for driving large nails. Its split peen or claw is used to lever bent nails out of the wood, which puts considerable strain on the shaft. A tough wooden shaft driven into a deep socket in the hammer head will be more than adequate for most purposes. Even stronger is a tubular-steel or fiberglass shaft permanently fixed to the head. A vinyl or rubber sleeve molded onto the shaft provides a comfortable non-slip handgrip.

Pincers
Small nails and panel pins are usually easier to remove with pincers, especially in confined spaces where it may be impossible to wield a claw hammer.

Cross-peen hammer

Continental-pattern cross-peen hammer

Pin hammer

Continental-pattern pin hammer

Claw hammer

Steel-shafted claw hammer

Driving nails with a hammer
Using a hammer of the correct weight, it should be possible to drive a nail in with the minimum of effort. Holding the tool near the end of the shaft, swing your arm from the elbow. Keep your eye on the nail and strike it square: glancing blows will bend the nail over.

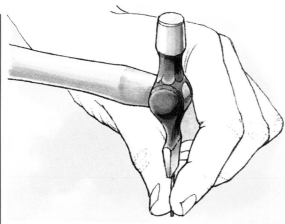

Starting a nail

When starting a nail, hold it upright between finger and thumb and tap the head with the hammer until the point is buried in the wood. Use a cross-peen to start a small nail or panel pin.

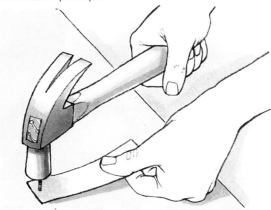

Supporting a panel pin

If you don't have a cross-peen hammer on hand, push a panel pin through a strip of stiff paper or thin cardboard, using it to hold the pin upright while you tap it into the wood. Once the pin is firmly embedded, tear the paper free and drive the pin home.

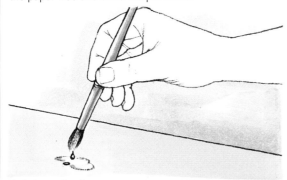

Raising a bruise

If you dent the wood with a misplaced hammer blow, apply a few drops of hot water to the bruise and wait for the fibers to swell. Once the wood is dry, you can sand it smooth.

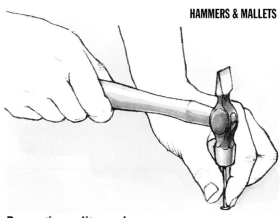

Preventing split wood

To prevent a piece of softwood from splitting, blunt the point of a nail by tapping it with a hammer. This makes the nail punch its way through the wood instead of wedging the fibers aside. When nailing hardwood, drill a pilot hole that is slightly narrower than the nail shank.

EXTRACTING NAILS

To draw a partially driven nail, slip the split peen of a claw hammer under the nail head, then use the shaft as a lever to extract the nail. To protect the surface of the work, slip a strip of cardboard or veneer under the hammer head. To draw an extra-long nail, substitute a block of wood for the cardboard or veneer.

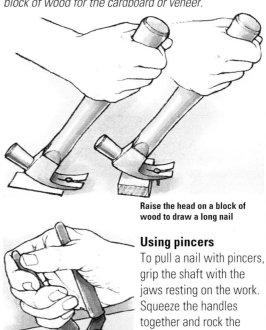

Raise the head on a block of wood to draw a long nail

Using pincers

To pull a nail with pincers, grip the shaft with the jaws resting on the work. Squeeze the handles together and rock the pincers away from you, protecting the wood from bruising with cardboard slipped beneath the jaws.

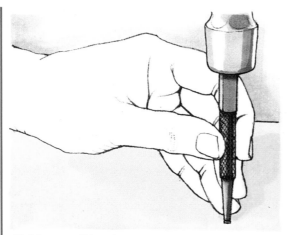

Sinking a nail head

To ensure that you do not dent the wood with the final hammer blow, drive the nail head flush or just below the surface of the work with a metal punch known as a nail set. Hammer the nail to within ⅟₁₆in (1mm) of the surface, then place the tip of the punch on the nail head, steadying it with a fingertip while you tap the nail set firmly with the hammer.

Secret nailing

Having buried a nail head as described above, you can cover it with filler before painting or polishing the workpiece. Alternatively, use a sharp gouge to lift a sliver of wood, then drive in the nail before gluing and clamping the sliver down to conceal the nail.

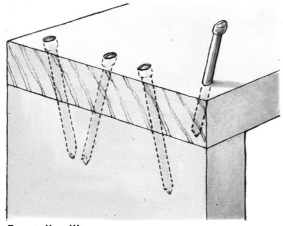

Dovetail nailing

Improve the grip of nail joints in end grain by inserting alternate nails at opposing angles.

MALLETS AND SOFT HAMMERS

A solid or laminated-beech mallet head is tapered so that swinging the mallet automatically presents the striking faces square to the work or to the butt end of a chisel. The socket within the head is also tapered to match the flared end of the shaft; with each swing of the mallet, centrifugal force tends to tighten the head onto the shaft.

Soft hammers and soft mallets have heads or striking faces made from rubber, plastic or coiled rawhide, which will not bruise the wood when dismantling or assembling frames and carcasses.

Carpenter's mallet

Rubber-head mallet

CHAPTER 9 To insert or remove a woodscrew successfully, it is essential to choose a screwdriver that fits snugly in the screw slot. To do otherwise is to run the risk of damaging the screw head or the work itself. Since there are a number of different types and sizes of screw slot, it follows that you are going to need a whole family of screwdrivers. One solution is to buy a power screw-driver with an extensive range of bits.

CHOOSING THE BEST SCREWDRIVER

There are several factors to consider before deciding which screwdriver will serve you best. The most obvious clue is the shape of the "slot" in the head of the screw. But how do you tell what type of cross-head screwdriver will fit an unidentified screw or what will be the best shape of handle for a particular job? Choosing the right size of tip to match a screw may seem obvious at first – but how does the woodworker match cross-head drivers to screw gauges, for example?

Cabinet screwdriver
The traditional-pattern woodworker's screwdriver is made with a bulbous wooden handle that nestles comfortably in the palm of the hand. Similar grips are now molded from plastic. Custom also dictates that the blade has a wide, flat heel that fits into a deep slot in the metal ferrule, but the cylindrical shaft on many a modern cabinet screwdriver passes straight through the ferrule into the handle.

Engineer's screwdriver
Screwdrivers with relatively slim, fluted handles were originally developed for the automotive and electrical industries. They are useful for delicate jobs where you might want to spin the handle with your fingertips, and their long parallel shafts are ideal for reaching a screw at the bottom of a deep hole. However, a parallel-sided handle with fluting does not provide as good a grip as a smooth bulbous surface when you want to deliver maximum torque at the driving end.

Stubby screwdriver
This short screwdriver with its wide tip and large handle is designed for driving screws in restricted spaces.

Ratchet screwdriver
With a ratchet screwdriver, you can insert or remove screws without changing your grip on the handle. A small thumb slide engages the ratchet for forward or reverse action; centralizing the slide immobilizes the mechanism so that the tool can be used as a conventional screwdriver.
The tip of a spiral-ratchet or pump-action screwdriver is driven clockwise or counterclockwise by applying straight pressure to the handle; the spring-loaded shaft extends each time pressure is released. The chuck takes special interchangeable straight-tip and cross-head bits.

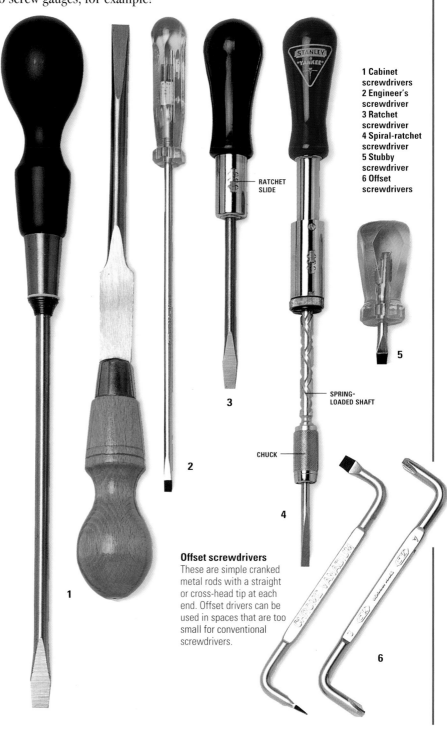

1 Cabinet screwdrivers
2 Engineer's screwdriver
3 Ratchet screwdriver
4 Spiral-ratchet screwdriver
5 Stubby screwdriver
6 Offset screwdrivers

RATCHET SLIDE

SPRING-LOADED SHAFT

CHUCK

1

2

3

4

5

6

Offset screwdrivers
These are simple cranked metal rods with a straight or cross-head tip at each end. Offset drivers can be used in spaces that are too small for conventional screwdrivers.

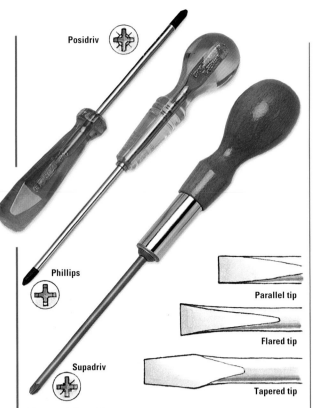

Posidriv

Phillips

Supadriv

Parallel tip

Flared tip

Tapered tip

Using a spiral-ratchet screwdriver

Steady the chuck with one hand while pumping the screwdriver with the other. If the screw feels too tight, remove it and rub the thread lightly across a bar of soap.

Screwdriver tips

Screwdrivers for straight-slot screws have either a parallel tip or a flared tip that is sometimes tapered by grinding away both edges. Some screwdrivers have pointed tips ground with four flutes to fit cross-shape slots. The main type of cross-head screw is a Phillips. Posidriv and Supadriv are less common. A Phillips screw has a simple cross, whereas the Posidriv cross has a small square at its center and can be identified by four narrow recesses that emanate from the center of the cross. A Supadriv screw has a similar cross with only two recesses.

 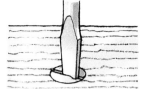

Matching tip to screw size

A screwdriver tip that is too wide for the slot will score the surrounding wood as the screw is driven home. If the tip is too narrow, it may not generate enough torque to loosen a stubborn screw but sufficient to gouge the metal on each side of the slot.

Cross-head screwdrivers are designated by point size: the chart below matches tip size to screw gauges.

Screw gauge	3–4	5–10	12–14	16 plus
Driver point	1	2	3	4

POWER SCREWDRIVERS

In-line cordless screwdrivers take much of the effort out of inserting woodscrews, especially in awkward corners where it can be difficult to produce the necessary turning force to drive a large screw flush. There is invariably a spindle lock, which is automatic on some models, so that you can use the tool manually to put the final turn on a screw or loosen it before you apply power. If the screwdriver is fitted with torque control, you have the option of a low setting to stop your overtightening of small screws or a higher setting for large fixings. When using a power screwdriver, it is just as important to keep the pressure on the tool when removing screws as it is when driving them home.

THREAD   SHANK   HEAD

Conventional woodscrews

The spiral thread of a woodscrew pulls it into the wood as the screw is turned. Only about 60 percent of a conventional woodscrew is threaded. The rest comprises a thick cylindrical shank (which acts like a dowel peg) and the head, which serves to clamp the workpiece or attachment in place.

THREAD   SHANK   HEAD

Twin-threaded woodscrews

The newer generation of screws has a double helical thread, which is relatively coarse and extends for almost the whole length of the screw. Because the shank is relatively slim, a twin-threaded screw can be inserted without the need for a clearance hole or even a pilot hole (see below), unless there is a risk that the wood may split when screwing into dense hardwood.

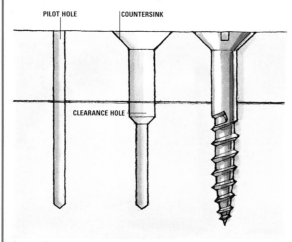

PILOT HOLE   COUNTERSINK

CLEARANCE HOLE

Inserting a conventional woodscrew

With brute force you can drive any screw into softwood, but in most circumstances it pays to drill a narrow pilot hole to guide the screw on its intended path and a wider clearance hole to prevent the shank from splitting the wood or jamming before you can drive the screw home.

Bore the pilot hole, using a drill bit that is slightly narrower than the threaded portion of the screw; then, to reduce friction, enlarge the first part of the hole with a bit that matches the shank diameter. If necessary, countersink the clearance hole before inserting the screw. (See also drill-and-countersink bits, pages 76–7.)

Counterboring a screw

If you need to drive a screw below the surface of a workpiece – to hold a deep rail in place, for example – bore a hole the same diameter as the screw head, using a Forstner bit or spade bit (see page 77), before you drill the pilot and clearance holes. Unless the joint is hidden below the work- piece, cover the screw head with a wooden plug (see pages 76–7).

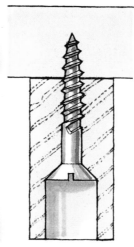

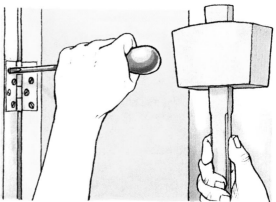

Removing woodscrews

Using a snug-fitting screwdriver with a large, comfortable handgrip, it should be possible to remove most woodscrews without too much trouble. However, an old screw may resist your initial efforts, especially if it has been in place for a long time or has been painted over at some time.

First, scrape any dried paint off the screw head and clean out the slot, then try tapping the butt end of the screwdriver with a mallet: the shock sometimes frees a stubborn screw. Alternatively, heat the head of the screw with the tip of a soldering iron, then try turning the screw again once the metal has cooled.

Repairing the tip of a screwdriver

A tip that has worn tends to ride out of the screw slot. Regrind each side of a straight-tip screwdriver, then grind the tip square. Replace a badly worn cross- head screwdriver.

CHAPTER 10 Portable machines take a lot of the drudgery out of sanding wood smooth, and a good finishing sander will produce a surface that to all intents and purposes is ready for finishing. However, for top-class work, examine a power-sanded surface to ensure there are no tiny scratches that will show up when you apply a clear finish. To be absolutely sure, it pays finally to damp the wood and rub down by hand.

BELT SANDERS

For a cabinetmaker, a belt sander used with a fine-grit paper will create a fine surface. However, a powerful belt sander can be a boon to the carpenter and is a handy bench-mounted machine for shaping workpieces.

Abrasive belts

A belt sander uses a continuous loop of abrasive-covered paper or cloth, held taut between a pair of rollers. An electric motor drives the rear roller, while the front one is adjustable to control the tension and tracking of the belt. A metal bed or "platen" mounted between the rollers holds the belt flat on the work. Sanding belts are between 3 and 4in (60 and 100mm) wide.

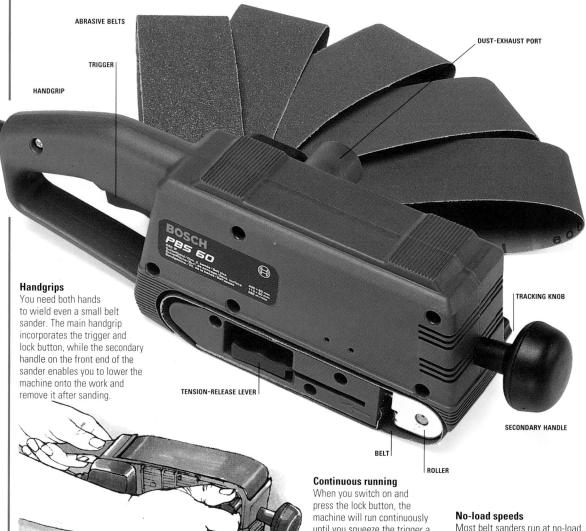

ABRASIVE BELTS

TRIGGER

HANDGRIP

DUST-EXHAUST PORT

BOSCH PBS 60

TRACKING KNOB

Handgrips
You need both hands to wield even a small belt sander. The main handgrip incorporates the trigger and lock button, while the secondary handle on the front end of the sander enables you to lower the machine onto the work and remove it after sanding.

TENSION-RELEASE LEVER

BELT

ROLLER

SECONDARY HANDLE

Changing a sanding belt
A torn or clogged belt can damage the surface of the wood, so discard a belt as soon as it begins to show signs of wear. Unplug the sander and pull the lever on the side of the machine to reduce the distance between the rollers so that you can remove a worn belt and replace it with a new one. Switch the machine on and adjust the tracking knob to center the belt on the rollers.

Continuous running
When you switch on and press the lock button, the machine will run continuously until you squeeze the trigger a second time. Continuous running can be an essential feature of power sanders.

Dust extraction
Belt sanding creates inordinate amounts of dust. All machines have a dust port for attaching a collecting bag; better still, connect your sander to an industrial vacuum cleaner (see page 105).

No-load speeds
Most belt sanders run at no-load speeds of between 617 and 1170ft (190 and 360m) per minute. On some models, electronic monitoring maintains optimum speed. If your work requires a more powerful machine, consider buying a professional-grade, variable-speed sander that has a top speed of around 1462ft (450m) per minute.

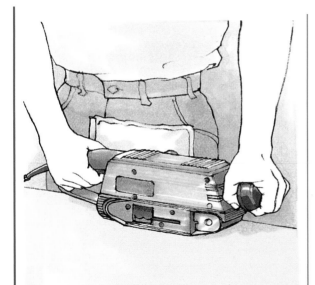

Using a belt sander

Switch on and gradually lower the sander onto the work. As soon as the belt touches the wood, allow the sander to move forward under control – holding a machine stationary for any length of time may score the work or sand a deep hollow. Move the sander across the surface, using parallel, overlapping strokes, following the general direction of the grain. Lift the sander off the work before switching off.

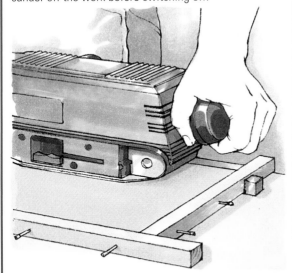

Sanding up to an edge

Take care to keep the platen flat on the work, especially as you approach the edges of a board or panel: if you allow the machine to tilt sideways at this point, you will wear away a sharp edge in seconds. With veneered boards in particular, take the precaution of temporarily pinning battens around the edges, flush with the surface, to prevent the sander from accidentally wearing through to the core.

BENCH-MOUNTED SANDERS

Clamping a belt sander to the bench leaves both hands free to control the work. A bench-mounting attachment includes an adjustable fence that helps you sand long edges accurately. Clamped on end or laid on its side, the sander can be used to shape workpieces. Change a belt as soon as the abrasive stops cutting efficiently, or you will scorch the end grain.

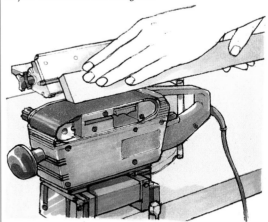

Run the work against the fence when sanding long edges

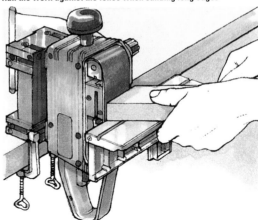

Clean up miters with the sander mounted on end

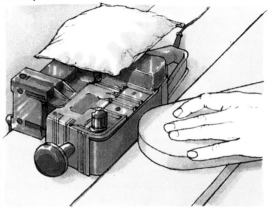

To shape workpieces, clamp the sander on its side

FINISHING SANDERS

Orbital sanders, designed to leave a smooth, flat and virtually scratch-free surface, have a foam-covered base plate faced with sheets of abrasive paper. Under power, the base plate describes a tight elliptical motion which removes wood relatively quickly but invariably leaves the surface covered with a pattern of tiny swirling scratches. Some machines can be switched to a straight reciprocal stroke to eradicate any visible scratches after the wood has been sanded flat.

Detail sanders
These are specialized orbital sanders with small triangular base plates, designed for sanding into tight corners and narrow rabbets.

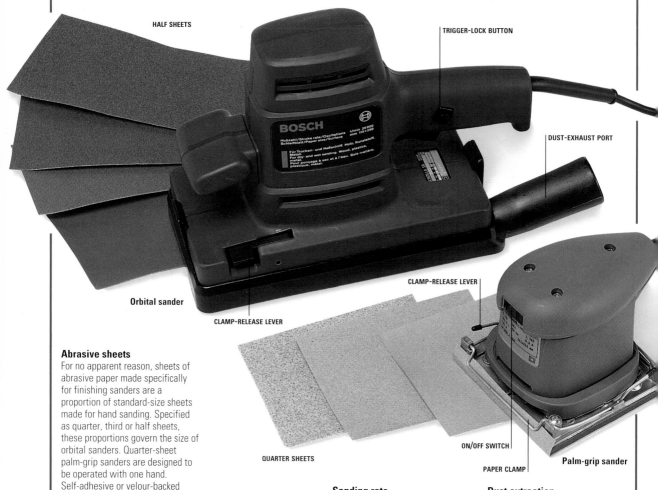

HALF SHEETS

TRIGGER-LOCK BUTTON

DUST-EXHAUST PORT

Orbital sander

CLAMP-RELEASE LEVER

CLAMP-RELEASE LEVER

QUARTER SHEETS

ON/OFF SWITCH

PAPER CLAMP

Palm-grip sander

Abrasive sheets
For no apparent reason, sheets of abrasive paper made specifically for finishing sanders are a proportion of standard-size sheets made for hand sanding. Specified as quarter, third or half sheets, these proportions govern the size of orbital sanders. Quarter-sheet palm-grip sanders are designed to be operated with one hand. Self-adhesive or velour-backed sheets of sandpaper can be peeled off the base plate when they need replacing. On other models, abrasive sheets are wrapped around the base plate and held in place at each end by a wire clamp.

Sanding rate
The sanding rate of orbital sanders is given as orbits per minute. Fixed rates of between 20,000 and 25,000opm are commonplace, but there are also variable-speed sanders which can be operated at much slower speeds for finishing heat-sensitive plastics and paintwork.

Dust extraction
Efficient dust extraction is not only desirable for your health, it also reduces clogging of the abrasive paper. On some models, the base plate and sandpaper are perforated so that the dust is sucked from beneath the sander directly into a collecting bag or vacuum cleaner.

Operating an orbital sander

Move the sander back and forth along the grain, covering the surface evenly with overlapping, parallel strokes. Keep the tool moving the whole time it is in contact with the work, and don't press too hard. Excessive pressure merely serves to generate heat, which causes wood dust and resin to clog the abrasive.

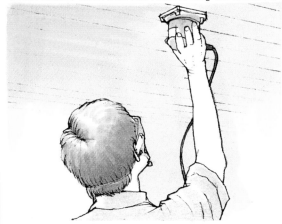

Working overhead

Even though it makes sense to choose the largest available machine when sanding sizable workpieces, you will find a lightweight palm-grip sander convenient for smoothing paneled walls and ceilings.

Cordless sanders

Very few manufacturers include a sander in their range of cordless tools, despite the obvious advantages of using a sander that has no electrical cord to get caught on the workpiece or other obstructions.

Abrasives for power sanding

A piece of wood is reduced to a smooth surface ready for finishing by gradually working through ever finer grades of abrasive grit that is resin-bonded either to paper or to fabric backing sheets. Aluminum oxide is widely used in the manufacture of sheets, belts and disks for power sanders. Silicon carbide, the hardest and most expensive woodworking abrasive, is another excellent material for sanding hardwoods, MDF and chipboard. Silicon carbide is also used extensively as an abrasive for rubbing down surface finishes such as paint or varnish.

Lubricants

Silicon carbide, in the form of traditional wet-and-dry paper, is lubricated with water to prevent the abrasive grains from becoming clogged with particles of paint or varnish. Abrasives are also coated with dry lubricants or stearates to reduce premature clogging with wood dust and finishes.

Antistatic additives

Antistatic additives included during the manufacture of bonded abrasives retard clogging dramatically and increase the efficiency of extractors. You may not be able to obtain ready-cut antistatic sheets for power sanders, but you can cut your own from rolls of a suitable width.

RANDOM-ORBITAL SANDERS

The random-orbital sander combines the characteristics of a disc sander with an eccentric orbital motion, which practically eliminates surface scratching. Some models have flexible sanding pads that can cope with curves as well as flat surfaces, but you need to switch to a detail sander to reach inaccessible corners.

DISK SANDERS

A bench-mounted disk sander is not meant to be used as a finishing sander. It is, however, extremely useful for sanding end grain and shaping workpieces. A rubber disk sander clamped in a portable power drill is classed as a finishing tool, but because it can leave deep cross-grain scratches this type of disk sander is really only suitable for relatively crude work, such as sanding floorboards. The soft-foam pads of miniature disk sanders conform to curved surfaces and uneven contours, making them especially useful to woodturners – and, since both the disk and lathe are moving simultaneously, you can remove tool marks quickly without leaving unsightly scratches across the wood.

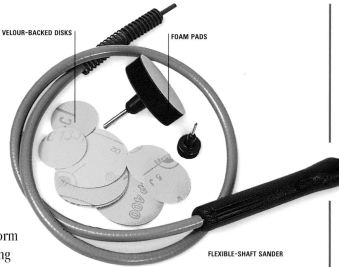

VELOUR-BACKED DISKS FOAM PADS

FLEXIBLE-SHAFT SANDER

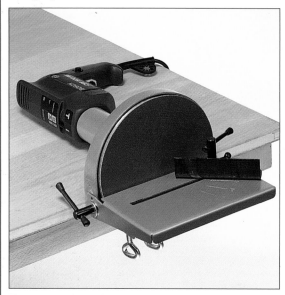

Bench-mounted disk sanders
Disk sanders are often manufactured as dedicated machine tools, but sturdy inexpensive power-drill accessories are also available. Each tool has a rigid circular backing plate to which you glue abrasive-paper disks. A metal support table, bolted across the plate, is adjustable to any angle from horizontal to 45 degrees and carries a fence that is used when sanding square ends and mitered workpieces.

Sanders may appear to be fairly innocuous power tools, but they can inflict very painful wounds, especially with coarse-grit abrasives. Don't switch on until you have made all the necessary adjustments, and keep your fingertips away from the moving disk.

Miniature disk sanders
Velour-backed abrasive disks are applied to arbor-mounted pads ranging from 1 to 3in (25 to 75mm) in diameter. Use an electric drill as a power source, preferably clamping the pads in the jaws of a flexible-shaft sander.

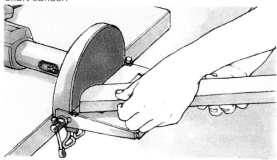

Shaping work on a bench-mounted disk sander
Saw a workpiece roughly to shape, then finish it by pressing the wood lightly against the left-hand side of the sanding disk: this ensures the rotating disk holds the workpiece firmly on the support table.

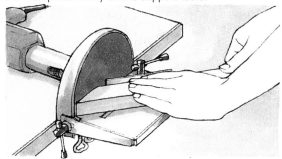

Sanding end grain and miters
With the fence adjusted to the required angle, slide the work up to the disk. Don't press too hard, or you will scorch the end grain.

CHAPTER 11

Cutting and shaping wood with a nicely honed chisel or plane is a pleasure; working with blunt tools is a chore. Sharp tools that cut easily and crisply not only leave a superior finish, requiring the bare minimum of sanding, they are also safer to use than those with dulled cutting edges that you have to force through a piece of wood.

SHARPENING TOOLS

WHETSTONES

A woodworking blade is kept sharp by using abrasive whetstones to wear the metal to a narrow cutting edge. The better-quality natural stones are expensive, but you can get very satisfactory results from cheaper synthetic stones. As part of the sharpening process, whetstones are lubricated with water or oil to ensure the steel does not overheat and to prevent fine particles of metal and stone from clogging the abrasive surface of the stone. Generally, whetstones are sold as rectangular blocks – bench stones – for sharpening everyday edged tools, or as small knife-edge or teardrop-section stones for honing gouges and carving chisels. Some discerning woodworkers prefer to sharpen blades on a diamond-impregnated stone or on a perfectly flat metal plate dusted with abrasive powder.

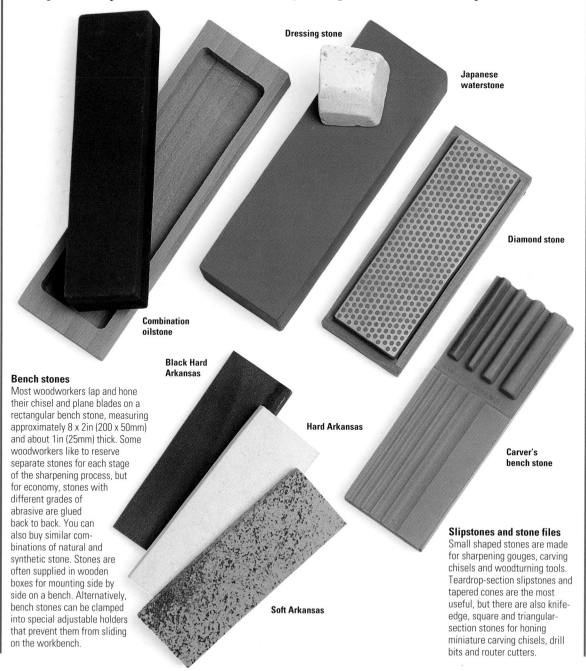

Dressing stone

Japanese waterstone

Diamond stone

Combination oilstone

Black Hard Arkansas

Hard Arkansas

Carver's bench stone

Soft Arkansas

Bench stones
Most woodworkers lap and hone their chisel and plane blades on a rectangular bench stone, measuring approximately 8 x 2in (200 x 50mm) and about 1in (25mm) thick. Some woodworkers like to reserve separate stones for each stage of the sharpening process, but for economy, stones with different grades of abrasive are glued back to back. You can also buy similar combinations of natural and synthetic stone. Stones are often supplied in wooden boxes for mounting side by side on a bench. Alternatively, bench stones can be clamped into special adjustable holders that prevent them from sliding on the workbench.

Slipstones and stone files
Small shaped stones are made for sharpening gouges, carving chisels and woodturning tools. Teardrop-section slipstones and tapered cones are the most useful, but there are also knife-edge, square and triangular-section stones for honing miniature carving chisels, drill bits and router cutters.

Oilstones

The majority of natural and man-made sharpening stones are lubricated with a light oil. Novaculite, generally considered to be the finest oilstone available, can be found only in Arkansas, USA. This compact silica crystal occurs naturally in various grades. The coarse, mottled-gray Soft Arkansas stone removes metal quickly and is used for the preliminary shaping of edged tools. The white Hard Arkansas stone puts the honing angle on the cutting edge, which is then refined and polished with Black Arkansas stone. Even finer is the rare translucent variety.

Synthetic oilstones are made from sintered aluminum oxide or silicon carbide. Categorized as coarse, medium and fine, man-made sharpening stones are far cheaper than their natural equivalents.

Waterstones

Because it is relatively soft and friable, a sharpening stone that is lubricated with water cuts faster than an equivalent oilstone: fresh abrasive particles are exposed and released constantly as a metal blade is rubbed across the surface of a waterstone. However, this soft bond also makes a waterstone vulnerable to accidental damage, especially when honing narrow chisels that could score the surface. Naturally occurring waterstones are so costly that most tool suppliers offer only synthetic varieties, which are almost as efficient.

Waterstones range from 800 grit at the coarse end, through 1000 and 1200 grits as medium grades, to something like 4000 to 6000 grits for final honing. Even finer, 8000-grit stones are available for polishing cutting edges. Extra-coarse 100 and 220 grits are used to repair damaged or very worn blades.

Chalk-like dressing stones are rubbed across the face of wet finishing-grade stones to raise a slurry that improves their cutting action.

Grade	Synthetic oilstones	Natural oilstones	Waterstones
Coarse	Coarse	Soft Arkansas	800 grit
Medium	Medium	Hard Arkansas	1000–1200 grit
Fine	Fine	Black Hard Arkansas	4000–6000 grit
Extra-fine		Translucent Arkansas	8000 grit

Diamond stones

Extremely durable coarse- and fine-grade sharpening "stones" comprise a nickel-plated steel plate that is embedded with monocrystalline diamond particles and bonded to a rigid polycarbonate base. These fast-cutting sharpening tools, available as bench stones and narrow files, can be used dry or lubricated with water. Diamond stones will sharpen steel and carbide tools.

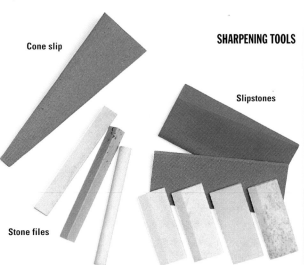

Cone slip

Slipstones

Stone files

Knife-edge slips

Metal lapping plates

Available as alternatives to conventional sharpening stones, oiled steel or cast-iron plates sprinkled with successively finer particles of silicon carbide produce an absolutely flat polished back to a plane or chisel blade and razor-sharp cutting edges. For the ultimate cutting edge on steel tools, finish with diamond-grit compound spread on a flat steel plate. Diamond abrasives are also used to hone carbide-tipped tools.

Caring for whetstones

Leave relatively coarse waterstones immersed in water for about five minutes before you use them; finer stones require less time. So that your waterstones are always ready for use, store them in fitted vinyl boxes to prevent moisture from evaporating, keeping the temperature above freezing. Keep an oilstone covered to prevent dust sticking to it, and clean the surface from time to time with paraffin applied with a coarse cloth.

Eventually, all sharpening stones become concave through constant use. Flatten an oilstone by rubbing it on an oiled sheet of glass sprinkled with silicon-carbide powder. Regrind the surface of a waterstone on a sheet of 200-grit wet-and-dry paper taped to a sheet of glass.

SHARPENING BLADES

A new plane iron or chisel is ground at the factory with a 25-degree bevel across its width. Some woodworkers like to hone this bevel to a sharp edge for working softwood; but, because the edge would be too weak to stay sharp for long when cutting hardwoods, it is usual to hone a secondary bevel – the honing angle – on a whetstone. The exact angle depends on the tool and the type of work you intend to do with it. A bench plane, for example, works best with a honing angle of between 30 and 35 degrees. A paring chisel, which should never need driving through the wood with a mallet, can be honed to an angle as shallow as 20 degrees, but cutting a mortise in dense hardwood might merit a chisel with a cutting edge honed to 35 degrees.

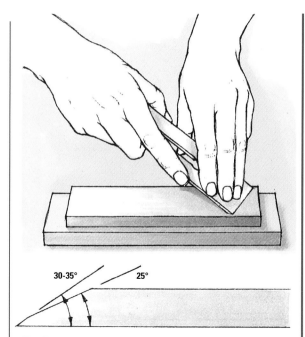

Lapping the back of a blade

Grinding a blade leaves minute scratches on the back and bevel, creating a serrated cutting edge that can never be truly sharp, even after honing. Consequently, the first stage of sharpening a new blade should be to flatten the back on a medium-grade bench stone or metal lapping plate.

Lubricate the stone and hold the blade flat on the surface, bevel-side up. Rub the blade back and forth, maintaining pressure with your fingertips to prevent the blade from rocking. Concentrate on the 2in (50mm) of blade directly behind the cutting edge – the rest of the blade can be left with a factory finish. Repeat the process on a fine whetstone until the metal shines.

Honing a plane blade

Grasp the blade, bevel-side down, with your index finger extended along one edge. Place the fingertips of your free hand on top of the blade, just behind the cutting edge.

Place the grinding bevel on a lubricated medium-grade bench stone, rocking the blade gently until you can feel the bevel is flat on the surface. Turn a wide blade to one side so that the whole of the cutting edge is in contact with the stone.

Tilt the blade up onto its cutting edge and rub it back and forth along the entire length of the stone to hone the secondary angle. Keep your wrists firm, in order to maintain a constant angle.

Honing a chisel

Sharpen a chisel exactly as described above – but, because most chisel blades are relatively narrow, move the cutting edge from one side of the bench stone to the other while honing to avoid wearing a hollow down the middle.

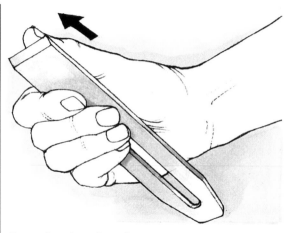

Removing the wire edge

Once you have honed a bevel about 1/32in (1mm) wide, continue with sharpening the plane blade or chisel on a fine-grade whetstone. Eventually the process wears a "wire edge" on the blade – a burr you can feel on the back of the blade with your thumb. Remove the burr by lapping the back of the blade on the fine stone, hone the bevel again with a few light strokes, and lap once more until the burr breaks off, leaving a sharp edge.

Stropping the blade

The final stage is to polish the cutting edge by honing on an extra-fine stone (see page 95) or a leather strop – a strip of thick hide lubricated with a small cake of fine stropping paste.

USING A HONING GUIDE

If you have trouble maintaining an accurate bevel when sharpening chisels and planes, try clamping the blade in a honing guide, a simple jig that holds it at the required angle to a whetstone. A honing guide, of which there are numerous different styles, is convenient for sharpening short spokeshave blades.

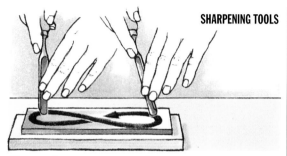

Sharpening an out-cannel gouge

To hone the edge of an out-cannel gouge (see page 72), rub the tool crossways on a bench stone, with a figure-of-eight stroke while rocking the blade from side to side. This brings the whole of the curved edge into contact with the stone and evens out the wear.

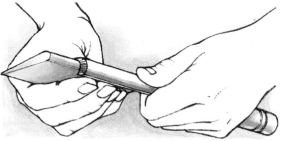

Removing the burr and stropping

Remove the burr raised on the inside of the blade with a lubricated slipstone. Finally, wrap the stone with a strip of soft leather to strop the edge.

Honing an in-cannel gouge

Use a similar slipstone to hone the bevel on the concave edge of an in-cannel gouge.

Removing the wire edge

Rub the back of an in-cannel gouge along a lubricated bench stone to remove the wire edge (see top left). Keep the back of the gouge flat on the stone while rocking the tool from side to side.

REGRINDING BLADES

It becomes impossible to work with blades that have worn unevenly, or when the cutting edge is chipped. Eventually blades have to be repaired by accurately regrinding the bevel to an angle of 25 degrees. You can repair a blade on a coarse bench stone, but because it is a somewhat slow and laborious task most woodworkers prefer to use a power grinder or motorized whetstone.

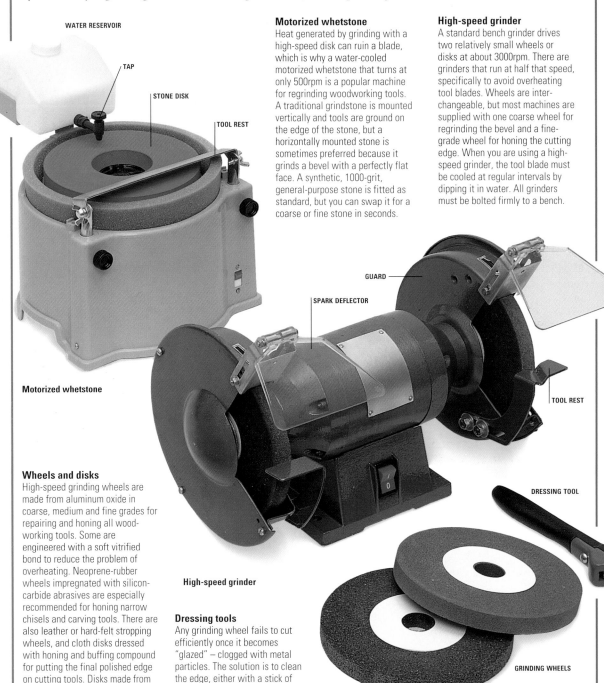

WATER RESERVOIR

TAP

STONE DISK

TOOL REST

Motorized whetstone

GUARD

SPARK DEFLECTOR

TOOL REST

DRESSING TOOL

High-speed grinder

GRINDING WHEELS

Motorized whetstone
Heat generated by grinding with a high-speed disk can ruin a blade, which is why a water-cooled motorized whetstone that turns at only 500rpm is a popular machine for regrinding woodworking tools. A traditional grindstone is mounted vertically and tools are ground on the edge of the stone, but a horizontally mounted stone is sometimes preferred because it grinds a bevel with a perfectly flat face. A synthetic, 1000-grit, general-purpose stone is fitted as standard, but you can swap it for a coarse or fine stone in seconds.

High-speed grinder
A standard bench grinder drives two relatively small wheels or disks at about 3000rpm. There are grinders that run at half that speed, specifically to avoid overheating tool blades. Wheels are interchangeable, but most machines are supplied with one coarse wheel for regrinding the bevel and a fine-grade wheel for honing the cutting edge. When you are using a high-speed grinder, the tool blade must be cooled at regular intervals by dipping it in water. All grinders must be bolted firmly to a bench.

Wheels and disks
High-speed grinding wheels are made from aluminum oxide in coarse, medium and fine grades for repairing and honing all woodworking tools. Some are engineered with a soft vitrified bond to reduce the problem of overheating. Neoprene-rubber wheels impregnated with silicon-carbide abrasives are especially recommended for honing narrow chisels and carving tools. There are also leather or hard-felt stropping wheels, and cloth disks dressed with honing and buffing compound for putting the final polished edge on cutting tools. Disks made from these relatively soft materials must be made to rotate away from cutting edges.

Dressing tools
Any grinding wheel fails to cut efficiently once it becomes "glazed" – clogged with metal particles. The solution is to clean the edge, either with a stick of silicon carbide or by abrading it with special diamond-tipped or star-wheel dressing tools.

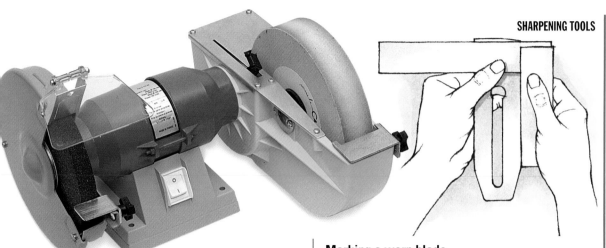

Combination grinders
There are machines that combine the advantages of high-speed grinding with slow whetstone sharpening. One common combination comprises a vertically mounted stone disk that runs through a bath of water at one end of the machine, coupled with the familiar aluminum-oxide wheel turning at a much higher speed at the other. Similar machines are manufactured with replaceable abrasive belts instead of a whetstone, or with a wide leather stropping wheel for honing blades.

Marking a worn blade
Before regrinding a chisel or plane blade, check the cutting edge with a try square. Use a fine felt-tip pen to mark a guide line square to the long edges of the blade.

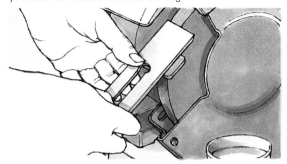

DRESSING A GRINDING WHEEL
A glazed grinding wheel cuts slowly and is much more likely to overheat woodworking tools. Wearing a dust mask and safety goggles, switch on the grinder and run a dressing tool or silicon-carbide stick from side to side across the edge of the wheel to clean the surface. The same process is used to reshape a worn or unbalanced grinding wheel.

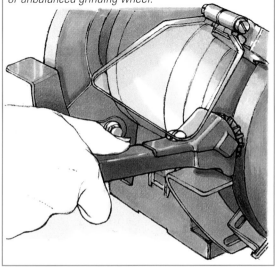

Grinding the blade square
Set the tool rest about ⅛in (3mm) from the edge of the grinding wheel, check that all clamps are tight, then switch on the bench grinder. Wearing eye protection, dip the tip of the blade in water and place it bevel downwards on the tool rest. Feed the blade steadily against the wheel, and move it from side to side as soon as the metal comes into contact with the abrasive surface. Dip the blade in water every few seconds to prevent the metal from overheating.

Regrinding the bevel
Once the blade is square, switch off and adjust the rest to present the blade at an angle of 25 degrees to the wheel. Switch on and grind the bevel across the width of the blade, keeping the metal cool with water.

SHARPENING SAWS

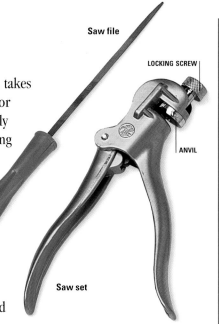

Saw file

LOCKING SCREW

ANVIL

Saw set

Reconditioning a saw, including topping, setting and filing the teeth, takes time to perfect, which is why many woodworkers send a saw away for professional treatment once it starts to jam in the kerf or consistently wanders off line. However, since the tools required for reconditioning saws are inexpensive and the techniques are simple in principle, there is no reason why anyone should not be able to achieve a satisfactory result with sufficient practice. In any case, it is not necessary to put a saw through the whole process each time you feel it is not cutting at its best. A few strokes with a saw file may be all that is required to put a blunt saw back into perfect working order. Sharpening is similar for handsaws and backsaws, except for those with hardpoint teeth which cannot be sharpened by hand. Small frame-saw blades should be discarded when blunt.

Saw set
This tool is designed to bend individual saw teeth precisely to the required angle. Squeezing the handles operates a plunger that presses each tooth against an angled anvil that is adjustable, to correspond to different-size teeth. The standard saw set copes with teeth up to 12 PPI; a fine saw set is also available. Some sets are made with a magnifying lens.

Saw file
The cutting edges of saw teeth are sharpened with a special triangular file. Each face of the file should be approximately twice the height of the saw tooth. Use the chart shown at upper right as a guide to selecting files for maintaining handsaws and backsaws.

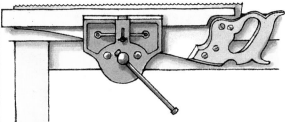

Clamping a saw
To prevent a saw from vibrating while being sharpened, the blade must be held rigid between stiff battens clamped just below the row of teeth. Cut a pair of hardwood battens long enough to support your largest handsaw, and shape them at one end to accommodate the saw handle. Sandwich the blade between the battens clamped in a bench vise; if necessary, pinch the battens together near the toe of the saw with a small C-

Selecting a saw file		
Saw	PPI	File length
Ripsaw	5–6	10in (250mm)
Crosscut saw	7–8	9in (230mm)
Panel saw	10	8in (200mm)
Tenon saw	13–15	7in (180mm)
Dovetail saw	16–22	6in (150mm)

USING A SAW-FILE GUIDE
Using a saw-file guide guarantees consistency of angle and depth when sharpening ripsaw and crosscut teeth. The jig fits onto the toothed edge of a saw, holding the captive file either square to the blade or at the appropriate angle.

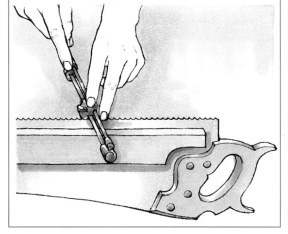

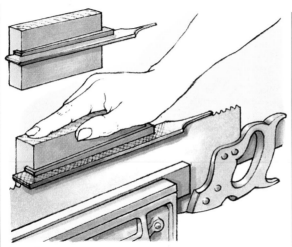

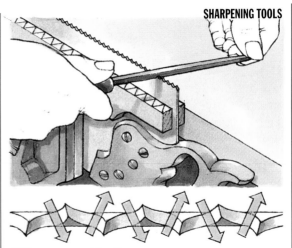

Topping a saw

Running a file lightly along the cutting edge of a saw puts a tiny bright spot on the point of each tooth. These will prove to be invaluable as guides to accurate sharpening. Topping is essential to reduce all the teeth to the same level when repairing a damaged saw.

Make a jig to carry a smooth metal file, by cutting a narrow tapered dado across a block of hardwood. Wedge the file in the dado. Rubbing the block against the face of the saw, make two or three passes with the file, covering the entire length of the blade each time.

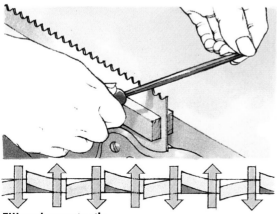

Filing ripsaw teeth

Clamp a ripsaw between battens, with its handle to your right. Starting near the toe of the saw, place the saw file on the first tooth bent away from you and against the leading edge of the tooth next to it. Steadying the file with both hands, hold it horizontal and square to the blade. Make two or three strokes, applying pressure on the forward pass only, until about half the bright spot on the tooth point is removed. Working towards the handle, place the file in alternate gullets until you have sharpened half the saw's teeth.

Turn the saw around and file the remaining teeth until the bright spots disappear.

Filing crosscut teeth

Sharpen a crosscut saw like a ripsaw, but turn the file to an angle of about 65 degrees to the blade, with the tip of the file pointing in the direction of the saw handle. Draw 65-degree parallel lines across the top of both clamp battens to help you orient the file.

Setting saw teeth

Adjust a saw set by releasing the locking screw on the end of the tool and turning the anvil until the required PPI figure marked on its edge aligns with the indicator. Retighten the screw.

Working from either end of the blade, locate the saw set over the cutting edge and bend each tooth that leans away from you. Turn the saw around and set the remaining teeth.

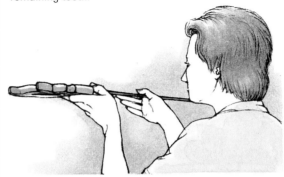

Checking the set

Hold the saw at eye level, with the teeth facing away from you, to check that you have not missed a tooth.

SHARPENING DRILL BITS

Although woodworkers are used to sharpening chisels and planes regularly, brace bits and twist drills tend to be neglected simply because a little extra pressure overcomes the problem of boring with blunt tools. However, a sharp drill bit works faster and makes cleaner, more accurate holes.

Sharpening brace bits
Sharpen center bits and auger bits similarly, using a small, flat, needle file.

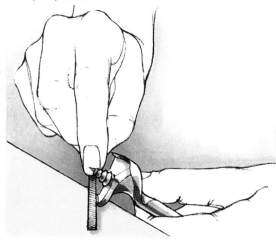

1 Filing the spurs
Start by stroking the inner face of each spur with the file. Don't under any circumstances try to sharpen the outer edges, because that would change the diameter of the bit.

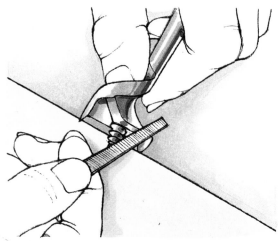

2 Sharpening the cutting edges
Holding the lead screw on the bench, file the bit's cutting edges. Take care not to damage the screw when filing.

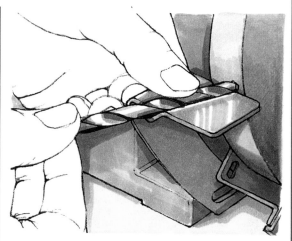

Sharpening twist drills
There are a number of brand-name sharpening jigs that hold a drill bit at the required angle to a small powered grinding wheel. Some sharpeners are designed for use with an electric drill, others have built-in motors. The better jigs, which will accommodate twist drills up to ½in (12mm) in diameter, are supplied with a standard aluminum-oxide wheel and another made from silicon-carbide for sharpening masonry drills.

You can also sharpen twist drills on a bench grinder (see page 98). Rotate the tip against the rotating wheel, making sure you grind both sides evenly to keep the point centered on the drill.

SHARPENING ROUTER CUTTERS
Sharpen router cutters by honing them on a whetstone or, in the case of carbide-tipped cutters, on a diamond stone or file. Rub only the flat faces on the stone, because to hone the outer edges could change the profile of the cutter. When sharpening two-flute cutters, treat each face equally. Remove the bearing before sharpening a self-guiding cutter; take care not to damage an integral pilot tip on the edge of the stone.

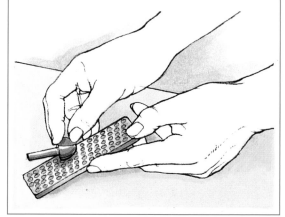

CHAPTER 12 For some, the kitchen table serves as an adequate worktop; but what dedicated woodworker would not prefer a special-purpose workbench in its own workspace, not least in order to avoid having to clear the decks at meal times? A solidly constructed workbench fitted with a sturdy vise makes every woodworking task easier and safer, especially when it has been installed in a well-laid-out and organized workshop.

HOME WORKSHOPS

Garages, outhouses and basements are commonly used as workshops. Ground-floor accommodation is preferable, particularly if your type of work requires the delivery of large boards, or you plan to install heavy machinery. Ideally the building should be separate from your house, in order to reduce noise levels and problems with permeating dust. However, the separate air-control and heating systems needed to provide the ideal working environment are more expensive to install in a remote workshop than if your house's existing systems can be extended.

1 Wall storage
Store handtools in wall-hung tool racks (see pages 114–15) within reach of the bench. For easy identification, fit narrow shelves to hold glass jars containing nails, screws and small fittings.

2 Electrical sockets
Install a run of double electrical sockets placed conveniently above the worktop.

3 Security
Fit locks to workshop doors and windows, not only to deter burglars but to keep children away from harmful chemicals and machinery.

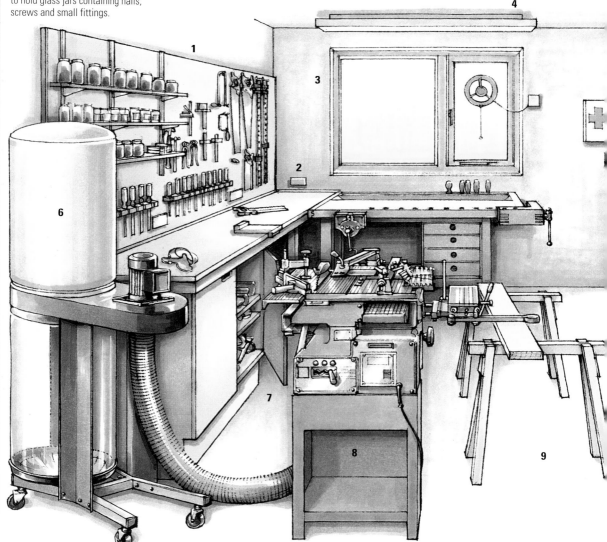

6 Dust extraction
To keep the workshop clean and reduce health hazards, connect a mobile dust extractor to your woodworking machinery.

7 Cupboard storage
Keep heavy handtools and power tools in a low cupboard.

8 Universal machine
If you have need for woodworking machinery but space is limited, install a unit that combines the functions of several machines.

4 Lighting

Where possible, site a work-bench adjacent to a window so you have good natural light. Paint the walls and ceiling white to improve the light level. Fit fluorescent lights to provide shadow-free illumination; use "daylight" tubes to help accurate matching of colors and veneers. Take care when using machinery, as fluorescent lighting can create the illusion that cutters are stationary.

5 Storing wood

If space allows, store man-made panels on edge between a specially constructed stud partition and a workshop wall. For easy access, position panel storage in line with the workshop door. Store solid wood and veneers on strong brackets bolted to the studs. Keep short offcuts in a drum container.

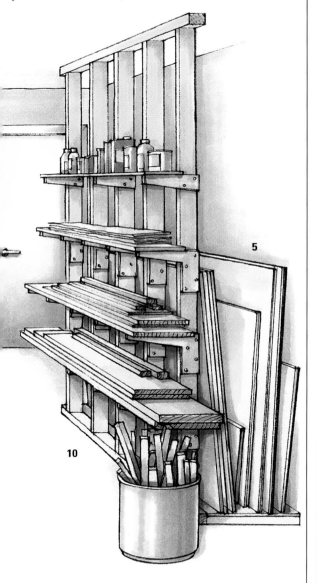

9 Assembly area

Try to keep an open space for assembly and finishing work, perhaps using a portable bench or sawhorses for support.

10 Open shelves

Store wood finishes and other materials on open shelving, but keep the bulk of inflammable materials in a separate shed. Place dangerous substances on a shelf that children cannot reach.

HEALTH & SAFETY

Sawdust and shavings left on the workshop floor constitute a fire hazard. The risk is increased when very fine dust is allowed to accumulate and float in the air, contributing to a potentially explosive atmosphere. To control the problem, purchase a dust extractor or an industrial vacuum cleaner that will remove the particles at their source.

Large-volume dust extractor

Industrial vacuum cleaner

Dust extractor

A mobile large-volume dust extractor is ideal for the small workshop. Dust sucked through a flexible hose is filtered from the air by a cotton bag, usually mounted on top of the machine, and collected in a sack below. The hose can be fitted with a variety of attachments for collecting dust directly from different types of woodworking machines.

Industrial vacuum cleaner

A heavy-duty vacuum cleaner, supplied with a range of hoses and nozzles, is useful for general workshop cleaning and can be connected to portable power tools for efficient dust collection at its source.

Safety equipment

Use plastic safety spectacles, goggles or a face screen to shield your eyes. Wear ear muffs or plugs when using machinery, particularly when working for prolonged periods. Use a mask or respirator to protect yourself from harmful dust and fumes; various types are available for working specific materials. Also, install a good-quality fire extinguisher, fire blanket and smoke detector in your workshop.

WORKBENCHES

There are numerous commercially made woodworking benches, available in various lengths and widths, but having a standard height of 2ft 8in (810mm); most manufacturers also supply made-to-order benches of any height. The cabinetmaker's bench has the most useful features, including two vises and some form of tool storage.

Scandinavian-style bench

Worktop
Most worktops are made from a tough, close-grain hardwood, such as beech or maple, though some are partly constructed from plywood. A composite construction is perfectly acceptable, provided that the top is thick enough and the surface veneer is able to withstand general wear and tear and periodic cleaning with a scraper. You may want to consider lining this type of worktop with hardboard that can be replaced at intervals.

Tool well
A shallow well is usually built into the worktop, enabling you to move a large workpiece or frame across the bench without sweeping tools onto the floor. Some benches are supplied with a separate tool tray that can be attached to the edge of the worktop.

Tool storage
A slot along the back edge of the workbench is convenient for storing saws, chisels and screwdrivers temporarily while work is in progress.

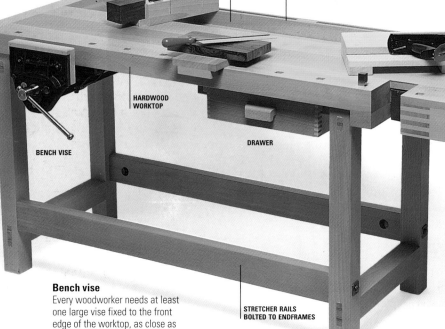

TOOL WELL

TOOL-STORAGE SLOT

HARDWOOD WORKTOP

BENCH VISE

DRAWER

END VISE

BENCH STOP

STRETCHER RAILS BOLTED TO ENDFRAMES

Cabinetmaker's workbench

Bench vise
Every woodworker needs at least one large vise fixed to the front edge of the worktop, as close as possible to one of the bench legs. This resists any flexing caused by forces applied to a workpiece held in the vise.

End vise
Better-quality benches are made with a second vise built into one end of the worktop.

Drawer
Most manufacturers offer the option of a single drawer for storing small tools, scraps of sandpaper, woodscrews and so on. Some provide a fully enclosed tool cupboard.

Underframe
When selecting a bench, check that the underframe is solid and stable, and does not twist when you apply sidewise pressure to the worktop.

Cabinetmaker's benches

Most benches are constructed entirely from hardwood, although less costly softwoods are sometimes used for the underframe. Underframes are usually constructed from two mortise-and-tenoned endframes joined together with stretcher rails that are securely bolted to the legs. This is a useful feature as it enables you to transport the bench more easily. A good-quality bench will have a worktop that is at least 2in (50mm) thick, invariably rectangular, with a vise at the side and at one end.

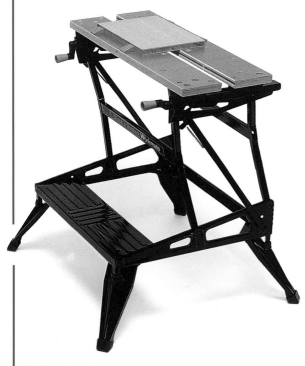

Folding bench

If you have no workshop or space is limited, you can buy a bench that folds flat for storage. It also doubles as a handy sawhorse in the workshop and as a portable bench for jobs around the house.

The worktop comprises two wide boards that form the vise jaws, one of which can be adjusted to grip tapered or parallel-sided workpieces by turning a cranked handle at each end. On some models, the same jaw can be set vertically to provide downward clamping pressure. Holes drilled in both halves of the worktop accommodate plastic clamping pegs which act as bench stops for gripping awkwardly shaped workpieces.

The metal underframe unfolds to standard bench height, but the splayed legs can also be folded under to provide a lower platform for sawing larger workpieces.

WOODWORKING VISES

Continental-style vises are made with thick wooden jaws to grip the work. Another type of vise has cast-iron jaws lined with wood to protect workpieces from bruising. Both designs are operated by turning a bar handle on the front jaw. Some metal vises are also equipped with a quick-release lever that disengages part of the screw mechanism, permitting the jaw to be opened and closed rapidly by a straight pull or push. (See also page 112.)

An end vise provides a clamping force along the bench to hold a workpiece between metal stops dropped into holes cut into the vise and at regular intervals along one or both edges of the worktop.

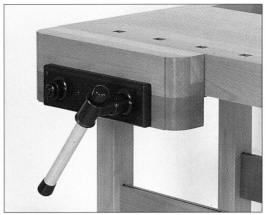

Continental-style vise

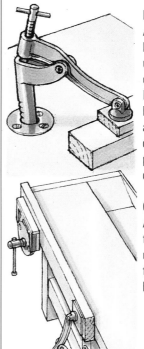

Holdfast

A holdfast is a removable bench-mounted clamp, used to hold a workpiece on the bench top. It has a long shaft that fits into a hole drilled into the top and lined with a metal collar; turning a screw presses a pivoted arm down onto the work.

Clamping a long board

A second collar fitted into the leg enables you to use a holdfast to support the end of a long board held in the bench vise.

CUTTING AND PLANING GUIDES

Cutting and planing guides are bench accessories that you can buy or make yourself. They are used for holding wood steady, and some guide the tool relative to the work. They also protect the bench top from tool damage.

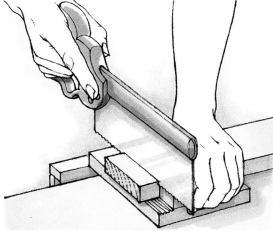

Bench hook

A bench hook is used to hold relatively small sections of wood that are to be cut to length with a backsaw. Hook the guide over the edge of a bench and hold the work firmly against the stop block while sawing. The baseboard supports the wood, to help prevent the wood fibers breaking out along the cut edge. Turn the guide over when the baseboard becomes worn.

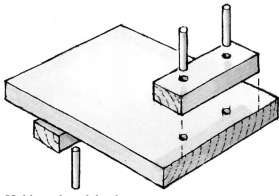

Making a bench hook

Cut a baseboard about 10 x 8in (250 x 200mm) from close-grained hardwood such as beech or maple, ¾in (18mm) thick. Cut two stop blocks 6in (150mm) long and 1½in (38mm) wide. Glue and dowel the blocks flush with the ends of the baseboard, on opposite faces. Inset the blocks by 1in (25mm) from each long edge; this enables the guide to be used by left- or right-handed woodworkers.

Miter box

This simple jig is for sawing miter joints, especially when joining lengths of molding. The box has two raised sides with slots cut in them to guide the saw blade. The central slot, cut square across the box, is useful for sawing to length strips of molding that are difficult to mark with a try square.

1 Making a miter box

Cut three 1ft (300mm) lengths of 3 x 1in (75 x 25mm) beech. Using one as a base, glue and screw the two sides to its long edges with their ends and edges flush. When the glue has set, mark the positions for the slots using a miter square and a try square (see page 20).

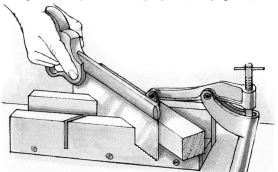

2 Cutting the slots

Clamp a 2 x 2in (50 x 50mm) guide batten across the box, flush with each diagonal line, and carefully saw the slots in the sides using a tenon saw held against the guide. Remove the batten and extend both slots down to the base. Cut the central, right-angle, slot in a similar way.

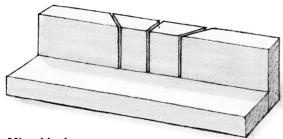

Miter block

A miter block is a simpler version of the miter box, having only one raised side, and is used in a similar way to a bench hook.

Shooting board

A shooting board is used to jig the work for planing end grain. Square and miter versions are available. The work is held against a stop block, which prevents the wood from splitting as a bench plane is slid along the jig to take a fine shaving.

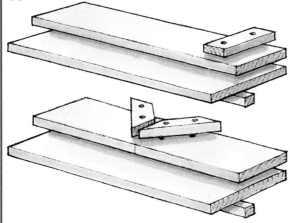

Making a shooting board

Cut a board 2ft (600mm) long from 9 x 1in (225 x 25mm) close-grained hardwood. Make a second board the same length from similar 6 x 1in (150 x 25mm) wood. Glue the boards face-to-face to form a step.

To make a square-cutting version, glue and dowel a stop block at one end, at right angles to the stepped edge. For a miter shooting board, fix two stop blocks in the center at 45 degrees to the stepped edge.

Fix a batten to the underside for clamping the jig in a vise. Alternatively, leave the underside flat and clamp the jig between bench stops.

SAWHORSES

Sawhorses provide a steady platform at a comfortable height for a variety of workshop tasks, but primarily for sawing planks and man-made boards. Having splayed legs, sawhorses can be stacked when not in use.

Making sawhorses

Cut a 3ft (900mm) length of 6 x 2in (150 x 50mm) softwood for the saddle. Make the legs from 4 x 2in (100 x 50mm) softwood. These are cut to length after assembly to give a working height of 2ft (600mm) from the floor.

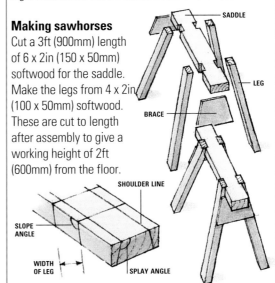

1 Marking the dadoes

The legs are set into the edges of the saddle, using compound-angled dadoes. Set a sliding bevel to 105 degrees and mark a sloping line 6in (150mm) from each end on both edges of the saddle. Hold the leg material on these lines and mark off their width at the same angle. Square these lines across the top and bottom.

Using the bevel, mark the splay angle on the ends of the saddle, inset 1in (25mm) from each edge at the top. Scribe shoulder lines parallel to the edges on the top and bottom, using a marking gauge set to meet the splay angle. Mark the waste.

2 Cutting the dadoes

Carefully saw down to the top and bottom shoulder lines, following the slope angle. Make a series of similar cuts about ½in (12mm) apart across the waste area. Chop out the waste with a chisel.

3 Fitting the legs

Glue and screw the legs into the dadoes, allowing their ends to project above the top surface of the saddle. Cut two braces from ½in (12mm) plywood to fit the angle of the legs and screw them in place.

When the glue has set, cut the legs flush with the top of the saddle. With the sawhorse standing upside down on a flat surface, scribe cut lines parallel to the floor at the required height and cut the legs to length.

MAKING A BENCH

A workbench must be both strong and rigid; a worktop that is able to flex or an underframe that can rock from side to side will absorb energy from the tools, making them less efficient and the work more difficult.

Make the bench as big as your workspace will allow, using stout sections of wood. If the workshop is solidly built, you could use the walls of the building as part of the structure – but a free-standing bench, which can be sited against a wall, offers a wider choice of work positions.

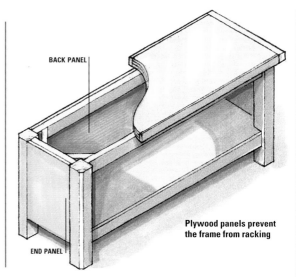

BACK PANEL

END PANEL

Plywood panels prevent the frame from racking

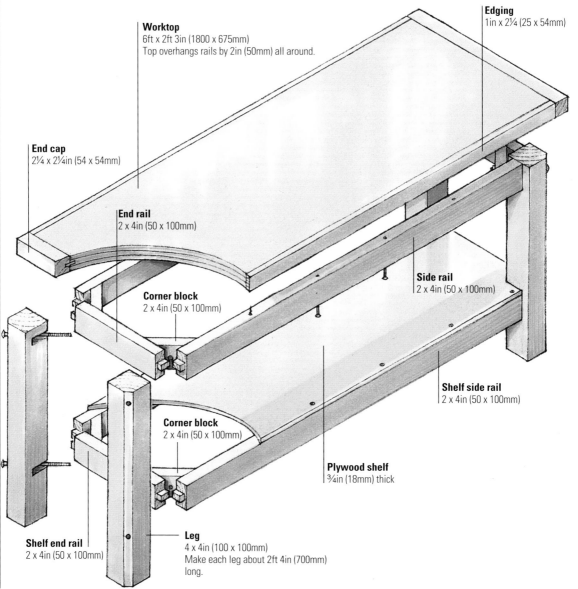

Edging
1in x 2¼ (25 x 54mm)

Worktop
6ft x 2ft 3in (1800 x 675mm)
Top overhangs rails by 2in (50mm) all around.

End cap
2¼ x 2¼in (54 x 54mm)

End rail
2 x 4in (50 x 100mm)

Corner block
2 x 4in (50 x 100mm)

Side rail
2 x 4in (50 x 100mm)

Shelf side rail
2 x 4in (50 x 100mm)

Corner block
2 x 4in (50 x 100mm)

Plywood shelf
¾in (18mm) thick

Shelf end rail
2 x 4in (50 x 100mm)

Leg
4 x 4in (100 x 100mm)
Make each leg about 2ft 4in (700mm) long.

Making a rigid structure

The rigidity of the frame relies to a large extent on the size of the material and the strength of the joints. You can buy plans for making a traditional cabinetmaker's bench or a modern interpretation of it. The plans are supplied with complete construction notes. Alternatively, make your own bench based on the design shown here.

To save money, make the bench using softwood framing and a laminated plywood top, in place of the hardwood used in commercially made benches. As with most workbenches, this design is made to be demountable; but here simple horizontal box frames, which form the top and lower shelf, are designed as the main structural members, with separate legs bolted to them. Extra rigidity can be provided by screwing plywood panels to the legs (see opposite).

Full-size drawing

Because the finished size of wood varies slightly from supplier to supplier, only the overall and nominal sizes are given. In order to work out the exact sizes for each component, make a simple full-size plan and elevation drawings of the leg joint, based on the size of your wood.

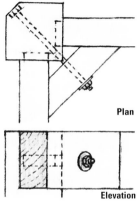

Plan

Elevation

Worktop assembly

Construct a worktop from three layers of plywood, ³⁄₄in (18mm) thick, glued together. Glue hardwood edging to the long edges, and cap each end with square sections. For additional strength, incorporate a stopped loose tongue in the end caps.

Side and end rails

Cut the side and end rails to length, including enough material for a stub tenon on each end. Cut the tenons back by ¼in (6mm) from the face of the rails. Screw the rails to the underside of the worktop. Glue and screw corner blocks on the

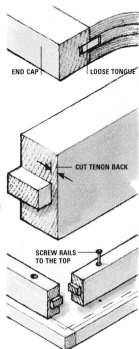

END CAP LOOSE TONGUE

CUT TENON BACK

SCREW RAILS TO THE TOP

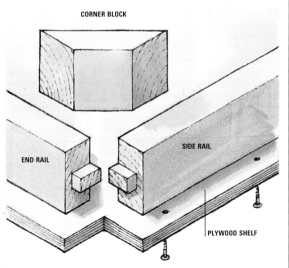

CORNER BLOCK

END RAIL

SIDE RAIL

PLYWOOD SHELF

Shelf assembly

Prepare the side and end rails as for the worktop. Cut the ³⁄₄in (18mm) plywood shelf to size and notch the corners to receive the legs. Glue and screw the shelf to the rails and fit corner blocks.

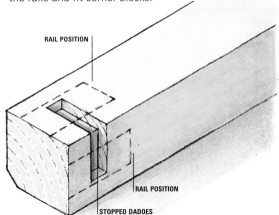

RAIL POSITION

RAIL POSITION

STOPPED DADOES

Making the legs

Cut the legs to length and chamfer the outer corner. Mark and cut stopped dadoes to receive the stub tenons on the two inside faces. Temporarily clamp the legs in place; then drill two counterbored holes followed by clearance holes, drilled diagonally through each leg and respective corner block, for an 8in (200mm) machine bolt. Fit the bolts with washers and nuts, then remove the clamps.

FITTING A BENCH VISE

The method for fitting a woodworking vise to a bench depends on how the rear wooden facing is fitted. The facing can be edge or flush mounted, the vise-jaw mounting bracket held in place with either coach screws or machine bolts. If bolts are used, the fixing holes will need to be drilled through the worktop and the bolt heads covered with wooden plugs.

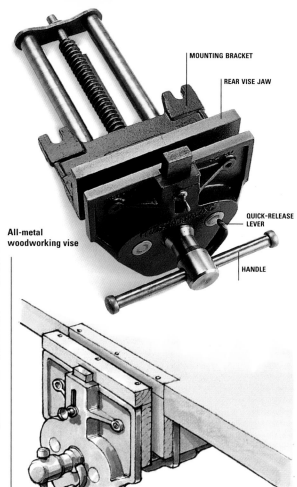

All-metal woodworking vise

MOUNTING BRACKET

REAR VISE JAW

QUICK-RELEASE LEVER

HANDLE

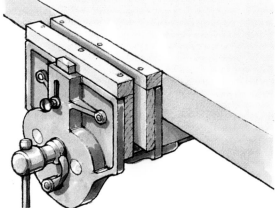

Edge facing
When the vise is fixed to the front edge of the bench, the projecting rear facing allows irregular-shaped workpieces to be more easily clamped in the vise without fouling the edge.

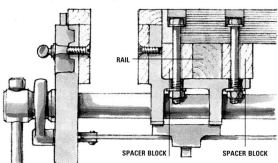

RAIL

SPACER BLOCK   SPACER BLOCK

Edge-mounting a bench vise
Make the front and rear facings from a close-grain hardwood cut not less than ½in (12mm) thick. Glue and dowel top cappings to the facings, and fix them in place with screws in the holes provided in the metal jaws. Cut a notch in the front rail of the bench to receive the vise-mounting bracket. Cut the depth of the notch to set the facings flush with the top surface of the worktop. Glue spacer blocks to the underside of the worktop to provide a level platform for the mounting bracket. Fix the vise in place with bolts or lag screws.

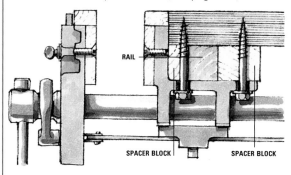

Flush facing
By setting the rear facing flush with the front of the bench, the edge of the worktop provides support for long, straight workpieces, clamped at the far end with an additional clamp or holdfast (see page 107).

RAIL

SPACER BLOCK   SPACER BLOCK

Flush-mounting a vise
Face the jaws as for edge mounting. Recess the front edge of the worktop to receive the rear jaw, so that the facing is flush with the edge. Notch the bench rail for the mounting bracket and fit spacer blocks as for edge mounting. Fix the vise with bolts or lag screws to the underside of the worktop. When using lag screws, mark and drill pilot holes in the blocks to aid assembly.

TOOL STORAGE

The sheer number of tools and materials used in a workshop, let alone the components produced, require good workshop discipline in order to avoid clutter, leading to poor work and possibly hazardous conditions. It is good practice to put tools away as soon as you have finished with them – and it helps if your tool storage is simple to use and, ideally, located within easy reach of the appropriate work area. Open racks offer easy access and quick identification, while enclosed cabinets provide tidy and secure storage.

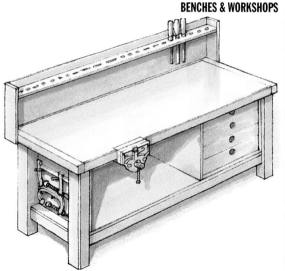

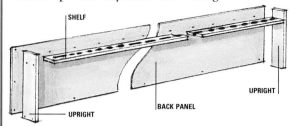

Bench-top tool rack

Construct the rack from MDF, 3in (75mm) wide by ¾in (18mm) thick, with a plywood back panel, ¼in (6mm) thick. Cut the back and side components to size so that, when fitted, the shelf will be about 1ft (300mm) above the bench top. Screw the plywood panel to the back edges of the uprights. Drill a series of holes and rout slots in the shelf to receive handtools such as hammers, chisels, screwdrivers and backsaws. Fix the shelf in place with screws through the ends and back. Mount the assembly on the back edge of the bench and fix it with woodscrews.

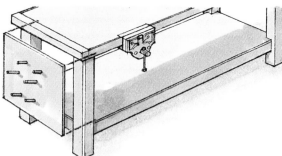

Making an end rack

Cut a panel of man-made board, ½in (12mm) thick, to fit between the bench top and the bottom shelf. After marking their positions, fix screw hooks or angled dowel pegs into the board, on which to hang the tools (see page 114–15). Screw the completed rack to the inside of the bench legs.

Benchside storage

Fitting tool racks and drawers to your bench will ensure that many of your tools are close at hand. The ideas shown here are intended for the project bench (see page 110), but could be adapted for other benches.

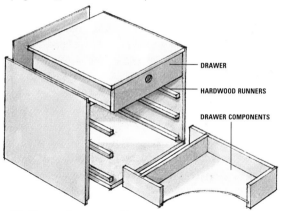

Making a drawer unit

The construction of the unit shown here uses simple dadoes and lap joints, but other methods of drawer making could be used. Make a box from ½in (12mm) plywood to fit the height and depth of the bench frame, to take drawers about 1ft 6in (450mm) wide. Calculate the number and height of the drawers to fit the box.

Fix ½ x ½in (12 x 12mm) hardwood runners to the sides, aligning them with pencil marks level with the bottom edges of the drawer fronts.

Cut and joint the main drawer components from ½in (12mm) MDF or plywood, as required to fit the box. Make the drawer bottoms from ⅛in (3mm) plywood. Drill a 1½in (38mm) hole in each drawer front for finger pulls. Glue and pin the components together; when the glue has set, sand and finish the wood.

113

WALL-MOUNTED STORAGE

For security and, to some extent portability, tools were traditionally stored in floor-standing chests, but wall storage is a more efficient use of space in a small workshop. There are many ways to attach tools inside cabinets or to wall-mounted back panels cut from stable man-made panels (see page 104). Select suitable methods from the examples illustrated here and opposite and, with these in mind, arrange your tools on a bench to find the most economical layout. If you intend to use pegboard wall panels with moveable hooks or clips, you can experiment with tool layout on the wall once the panels are in place. Whatever methods you adopt, use strong materials such as plywood, MDF or close-grained hardwood to make racks and supports for individual tools or complete sets.

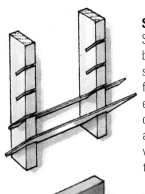

Slotted uprights
Screw-fixed uprights can be used to store cabinet scrapers, metal rules and files; and if made large enough, to carry sash cramps. Cut the slots at an angle of about 45 degrees; width of slot depends on the tool in question.

Slotted ledges
A simple wooden ledge with a slot cut in one end will support and hold measuring-and-marking tools such as sliding bevels and try squares.

Lipped ledges
Plain lipped ledges can be used to support and secure a variety of tools, such as try squares, braces, coping saws and other types of frame saw (see page 37). This type of support can also be adapted for holding bench planes. Make a pair of ledges, one with a deep edging that is notched to fit around the round knob or horn near the toe of the plane. Fix one ledge above the other, with the upper one inverted, allowing sufficient space between them to lift out the plane.

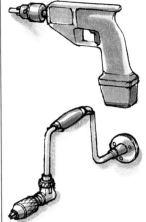

Angled pegs
Wooden dowel pegs, used singly or in pairs or rows, can be adapted to support a wide range of tools. Use a relatively thick back panel for this method and drill holes at an angle of 5 degrees to receive short dowels of ¼, ⅜ or ½in (6, 9 or 12mm) diameter, depending on the size or weight of the tool.

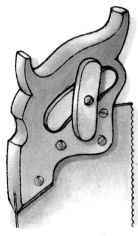

Turn buttons
Use turn buttons to support and secure saws by their handles. Draw around the inside of the saw handle to get the shape of the fixed block and pivoting button. Make the fixed block slightly thicker than the handle, and the button from ¼in (6mm) plywood. Fit the button to the center of the block with a screw.

Drilled blocks
Drilled blocks offer secure support for drill bits and router cutters. If you make a stepped block, each row of bits or cutters will be easier to see and handle.

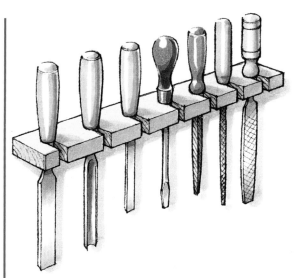

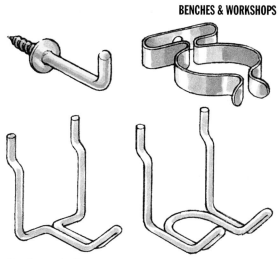

Drilled-and-slotted rails

Use these for storing straight-handled tools such as chisels, screwdrivers and files. Drill a series of holes to accommodate the ferrule at the base of each handle, and cut a slot from the edge of the rail into the hole to aid in removal of the tool. Glue and screw the rail to the back panel.

Hooks and clips

Metal screwhooks can be driven into a rigid back panel, and spring clips are made in a range of sizes to hold various tools. You can also buy hooks that plug into ready-made panels. Alternatively, make your own fittings for use with perforated hardboard, known as pegboard. Make single or double hooks from coat-hanger wire.

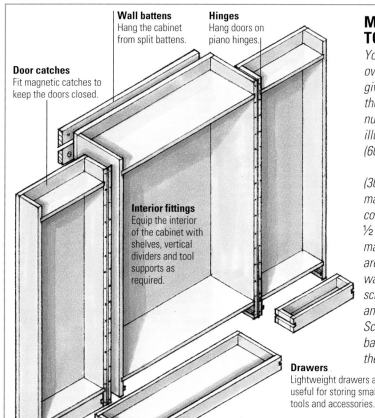

Wall battens
Hang the cabinet from split battens.

Hinges
Hang doors on piano hinges.

Door catches
Fit magnetic catches to keep the doors closed.

Interior fittings
Equip the interior of the cabinet with shelves, vertical dividers and tool supports as required.

Drawers
Lightweight drawers are useful for storing small tools and accessories.

MAKING A WALL-HUNG TOOL CABINET

You can design a tool cabinet to suit your own requirements using the dimensions given here as a guide. The overall size of the cabinet will depend on the type and number of tools being stored, but the one illustrated here is 3ft (900mm) high by 2ft (600mm) wide.

The depth should not exceed 1ft (300mm) when closed. To improve access, make the doors as fold-back storage compartments. Construct the cabinet from ½ or ⅝in (12 or 16mm) MDF or similar man-made board. The small "drawers" are optional. Hang the cabinet from the wall on 45-degree split battens, one screwed to the wall, the other screwed and glued to the back of the cabinet. Screw a similar spacer batten near the base of the cabinet to keep it away from the wall.

PORTABLE TOOL STORAGE

Most woodworkers find it is easier to produce their best work in a properly equipped workshop, but there are times when it is more convenient, or perhaps necessary, to take the tools to the work. Some form of portable storage such as a tote box, tool bag or carpenter's tool belt will suffice, provided the cutting edges of saws, chisels and other tools are protected. Pocketed canvas rolls are available for sets of chisels and large drill bits. For saws, you can purchase a tailored fabric saw case, but covering their teeth with plastic spine-binder clips made for paper or a slotted wooden batten held with elastic cord are cheaper alternatives.

Belts with leather pouches carry a variety of handtools

Dividers
Fit partitions as required.

Carrying handle
Glue steel tube at each end to form a strong handle.

End and side panels
Pin and glue butt-jointed panels.

Tray handles
Notch each support batten to form a handle.

Lift-out tray
Make divided tray to fit tote box.

Plywood tote box

Tool bags

Canvas and leather tool bags are made with reinforced bottoms and strong carrying handles. Available in various sizes, they have fitted pockets that help protect tools from accidental damage and make it easier to locate smaller tools and accessories. A shoulder strap is an advantage when carrying a fully loaded bag.

Tool belts

A handy tool belt enables you to carry essential tools right to the work site, even if you have to climb a ladder. Some belts or holsters are designed to hold individual tools, such as a claw hammer or power drill, but one that has pockets for nails and screws as well as various-size loops for hammers, screwdrivers or squares is more versatile.

Tote boxes

You can buy metal or plastic mechanic's tool boxes fitted with trays which, so long as your cutting-edge tools are wrapped or sleeved, are suitable for woodworking tools. Alternatively, make an open-topped tote box with a lift-out tray for smaller tools. Basing it on the design shown here, make the box from plywood to suit your own requirements. Depending on the size,the box can also be used as a makeshift sawhorse or, with a strong board laid across it, as an occasional step-up.

CHAPTER *13*

Although Japanese tools are used quite differently from conventional saws, planes and chisels, European and American woodworkers have taken enthusiastically to these unfamiliar tools. Due in part to the almost legendary skills that go into their manufacture, Japanese tools have acquired a reputation for quality among collectors and woodworkers alike.

JAPANESE SAWS

Because Japanese saws are designed to cut on the pull stroke, they can be made with blades that are thinner than their Western equivalents. Since their teeth are also finely set, these saws are capable of cutting relatively narrow kerfs. The best blades are taper ground to reduce friction, and the straight wooden handles are often bound with split bamboo.

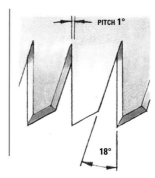

PITCH 1°

18°

Japanese crosscut teeth
The Japanese crosscut tooth is taller and narrower than the Western version, and also has a third bevel filed across the top. Some manufacturers have adopted this style of tooth for conventional handsaws that cut on the forward stroke.

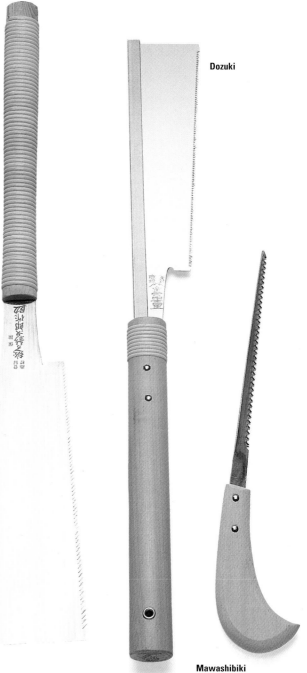

Kataba

Dozuki

Ryoba

Mawashibiki

Kataba
A kataba is similar to a Western handsaw in that it has a row of crosscut or ripsaw teeth along one edge of a broad blade that helps keep the saw on course.

Ryoba
A ryoba is a combination saw with crosscut teeth along one edge and ripsaw teeth along the other. It is convenient to be able to cut a workpiece to length and width without having to change saws, but the blade of a ryoba has to be held at a relatively shallow angle to prevent the uppermost row of teeth from scoring the sides of the kerf. Consequently, you may have to sever a thick piece of wood by sawing from all four sides.

Dozuki
The dozuki is the Japanese equivalent of the backsaw. The dovetail version, with about 23 PPI, has a narrow blade that cuts an extremely fine kerf with virtually no tearing of the grain. The teeth are graded in size towards the heel of the saw, for starting the cut.

Mawashibiki
The mawashibiki, with its narrow tapered blade, has much in common with the familiar compass saw (see page 37), but there is less danger of buckling a blade that cuts on the back stroke.

PLANES

A Japanese woodworking plane comprises a simple hardwood body that accommodates a laminated-steel blade and a cap iron, which breaks and curls the shavings to prevent the wood fibers from tearing in advance of the blade. A steel retaining pin keeps the cap iron pressed against the blade. Although these tools are not dissimilar to traditional Western bench planes and molding planes, the Japanese technique for planing wood is quite distinctive. Japanese woodworkers plane backwards and, with a finely set tool, will cut a continuous wafer-thin shaving from one end of a workpiece to the other.

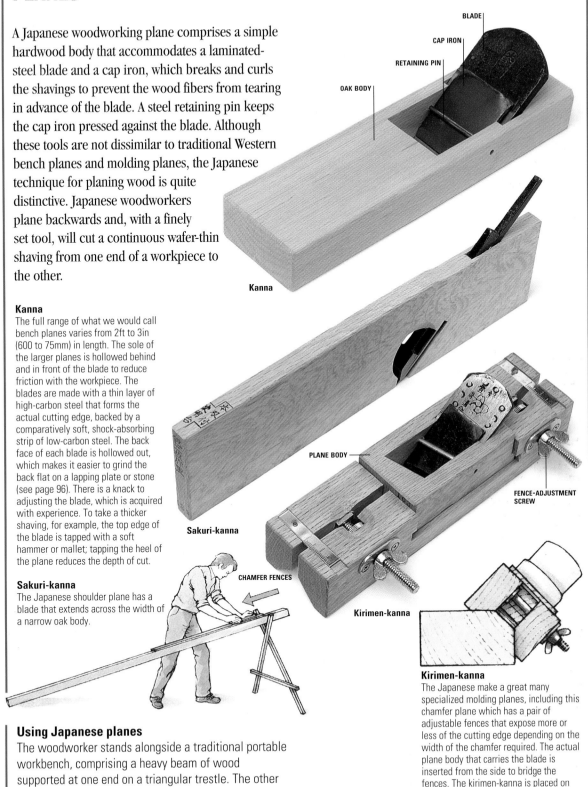

BLADE
CAP IRON
RETAINING PIN
OAK BODY

Kanna

PLANE BODY

Sakuri-kanna

FENCE-ADJUSTMENT SCREW

CHAMFER FENCES

Kirimen-kanna

Kanna
The full range of what we would call bench planes varies from 2ft to 3in (600 to 75mm) in length. The sole of the larger planes is hollowed behind and in front of the blade to reduce friction with the workpiece. The blades are made with a thin layer of high-carbon steel that forms the actual cutting edge, backed by a comparatively soft, shock-absorbing strip of low-carbon steel. The back face of each blade is hollowed out, which makes it easier to grind the back flat on a lapping plate or stone (see page 96). There is a knack to adjusting the blade, which is acquired with experience. To take a thicker shaving, for example, the top edge of the blade is tapped with a soft hammer or mallet; tapping the heel of the plane reduces the depth of cut.

Sakuri-kanna
The Japanese shoulder plane has a blade that extends across the width of a narrow oak body.

Using Japanese planes
The woodworker stands alongside a traditional portable workbench, comprising a heavy beam of wood supported at one end on a triangular trestle. The other end of the beam butts against a wall or tree trunk. The plane is pulled backwards along the workpiece.

Kirimen-kanna
The Japanese make a great many specialized molding planes, including this chamfer plane which has a pair of adjustable fences that expose more or less of the cutting edge depending on the width of the chamfer required. The actual plane body that carries the blade is inserted from the side to bridge the fences. The kirimen-kanna is placed on the corner of the workpiece, with one fence running against each face.

CHISELS & GOUGES

As with plane blades, a laminated-steel construction is used for the manufacture of Japanese chisels. The hollow-ground blade, socket and tang are forged in one piece, forming the strongest possible joint with the hardwood handle, which is also reinforced with a deep, tapered ferrule.

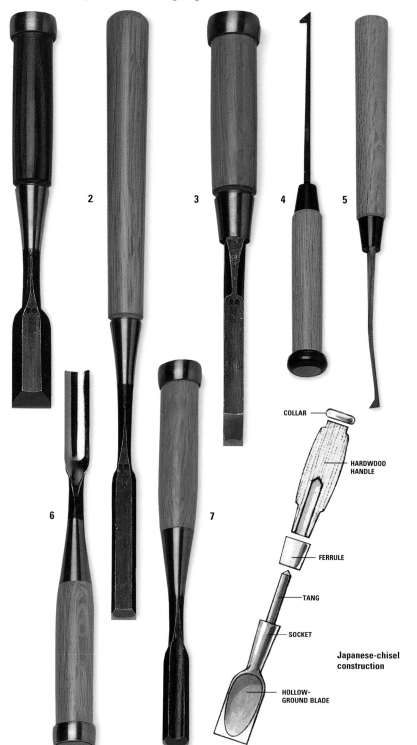

1 Oiri-nomi
The oiri-nomi is the Japanese equivalent of the firmer chisel. It is strong enough to be driven with a mallet, despite having a bevel-edged blade.

2 Usu-nomi
The comparatively lightweight usu-nomi is a paring chisel designed to be used with a two-handed grip.

3 Mukomachi-nomi
The mukomachi-nomi is very similar to a Western mortise chisel, having a thick rectangular-section blade for cutting deep recesses.

4 Moro-nomi and
5 Sokozarai-nomi
These specialized chisels, used to clean up the sides and bottom of a mortise, are made with hooks for clearing out the waste.

6 Uchi-hagane-nomi
In common with chisels that are mallet-driven, the Japanese out-cannel firmer gouge is fitted with a metal collar that prevents the handle from splitting.

7 Oiri-uramaru-nomi
The in-cannel gouge, made for scribing rounded shoulders, has a thick blade ground with a flat bevel.

COLLAR

HARDWOOD HANDLE

FERRULE

TANG

SOCKET

Japanese-chisel construction

HOLLOW-GROUND BLADE

CHAPTER 14 The capacity to execute a fine piece of carving goes beyond pure technique, but the ability to handle specialized woodcarving tools is without doubt the first requirement. This chapter is an introduction to the extensive range of chisels, gouges and other handtools that are made for carving fully three-dimensional forms and low-relief decoration.

CARVER'S TOOLS

CARVING CHISELS & GOUGES

It might seem unnecessary to acquire a whole new set of woodcarving tools when you could use your standard firmer chisels and gouges, but specialized carving tools are generally beveled on both sides of the blade to facilitate cutting the wood at a variety of angles. Chisels have equal bevels ground on each side of the cutting edge, whereas gouges and parting tools have a larger bevel on the outside of the blade. In common with other woodworking tools, carving chisels and gouges are sold with cutting edges ground but not sharpened.

The standard range of chisels and gouges can include up to 10 different cutting-edge profiles, with a choice of five shapes of blade and a wide range of sizes. However, a few basic tools are sufficient as a starter kit.

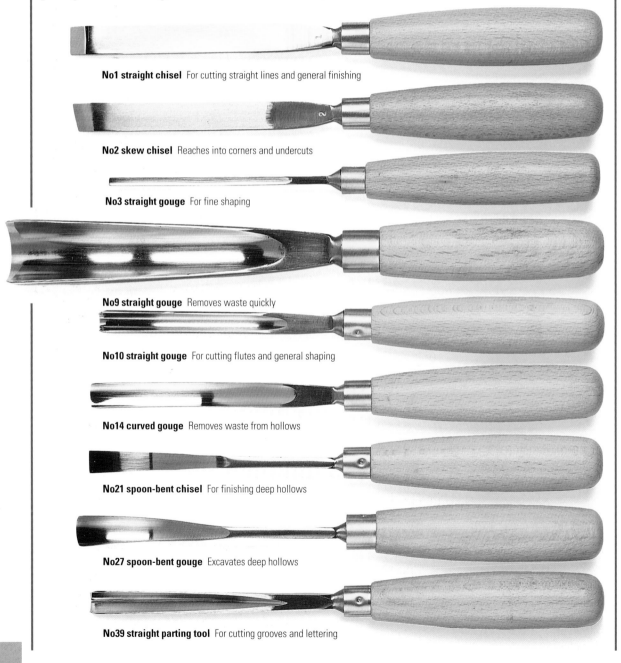

No1 straight chisel For cutting straight lines and general finishing

No2 skew chisel Reaches into corners and undercuts

No3 straight gouge For fine shaping

No9 straight gouge Removes waste quickly

No10 straight gouge For cutting flutes and general shaping

No14 curved gouge Removes waste from hollows

No21 spoon-bent chisel For finishing deep hollows

No27 spoon-bent gouge Excavates deep hollows

No39 straight parting tool For cutting grooves and lettering

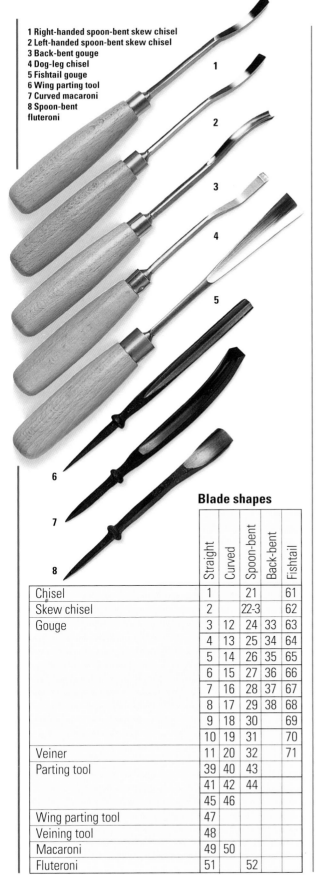

1 Right-handed spoon-bent skew chisel
2 Left-handed spoon-bent skew chisel
3 Back-bent gouge
4 Dog-leg chisel
5 Fishtail gouge
6 Wing parting tool
7 Curved macaroni
8 Spoon-bent
fluteroni

1
2
3
4
5
6
7
8

CARVER'S TOOLS

CHISEL
SKEWED CHISEL
GOUGES
VEINER
PARTING TOOLS
90°
60°
45°
WING PARTING TOOL
VEINING TOOL
MACARONI
FLUTERONI

STRAIGHT
CURVED
SPOON-BENT
BACK-BENT
DOG-LEG
FISHTAIL

Cutting profiles

Carving tools are made with a variety of cutting-edge profiles, all designed for different purposes. The majority are either chisels or gouges used for waste removal and general shaping. Some chisels are skewed for cutting into acute corners. Veiners and veining tools are deep-sided gouges, and V-shape parting tools are used for cutting grooves and for outlining lettering. You can get 90-, 60- and 45-degree parting tools, and there is also a shallow wing parting tool with curved sides. The macaroni and fluteroni are rectangular-section gouges for cutting flat-bottomed hollows or recesses. A macaroni has sharp square corners, whereas the corners of a fluteroni are rounded.

Blade shapes

You can buy straight-bladed carving tools with their various cutting profiles. A great many of them are also available with blades that are curved for carving hollows and undercuts; spoon-bent and back-bent tools are deeply curved towards the tip of the blade. Dog-leg tools have cranked blades, and fishtail tools have straight blades with splayed tips.

Blade shapes

	Straight	Curved	Spoon-bent	Back-bent	Fishtail
Chisel	1		21		61
Skew chisel	2		22-3		62
Gouge	3	12	24	33	63
	4	13	25	34	64
	5	14	26	35	65
	6	15	27	36	66
	7	16	28	37	67
	8	17	29	38	68
	9	18	30		69
	10	19	31		70
Veiner	11	20	32		71
Parting tool	39	40	43		
	41	42	44		
	45	46			
Wing parting tool	47				
Veining tool	48				
Macaroni	49	50			
Fluteroni	51		52		

Numbering system

Most tool suppliers use the recognized numbering system, which helps to identify a particular combination of cutting-edge profile and blade shape (see chart at left). Numbers 3 to 10, for example, designate the group of straight gouges, with cutting edges that range from an almost flat profile to semi-circular. Gouges 12 to 19 feature exactly the same range of profiles but with curved blades. Chisels and most gouges range from 1/16 to 2in (2 to 50mm) in width. Some of the more specialized carving tools are available in fewer sizes.

USING CHISELS & GOUGES

Woodcarving technique differs from most methods of working wood in that carving cuts are generally made across the grain. This is particularly true when using gouges to remove the waste for "roughing out" a piece of work, where the wood may be cut from practically any angle. Provided the tools are kept razor sharp, even relatively deep cuts will not split the wood as could easily happen when working parallel with the grain. When it comes to finishing cuts, it pays to study grain direction closely to ensure the areas you want to preserve are cut cleanly. For example, a gouged cut made diagonally across the grain leaves a groove that is clean cut on one side but is slightly rougher on the other, where it runs against the grain.

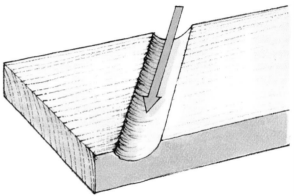

A diagonal cut is smoother on one side than on the other

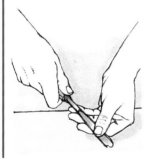

Making heavy paring cuts

The essence of any carving technique is control over the depth and angle of the cut. When making fairly deep cuts, nestle the end of the handle in the palm of your hand and extend the forefinger along the blade. With this grip you can apply pressure to the tool and control the direction of cut by twisting your wrist.

Control the speed of cut with your other hand; gripping the blade provides resistance to the forward movement. With your wrist resting on the work surface, you can also change the angle of the tool.

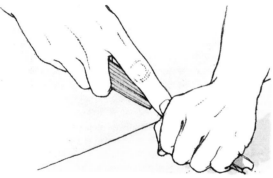

Making light cuts

When making shallow finishing cuts, ensure delicate control over the tool by pinching the blade between forefinger and thumb, with your knuckles resting on the work.

Making vertical cuts

To make a vertical cut, grip the tool handle in one hand, with your thumb curled over the end. Guide and control the tool with your other hand, gripping the blade between finger and thumb.

USING A CARVER'S MALLET

When removing a lot of waste or when working particularly dense wood, it is sometimes necessary to drive carving tools with a mallet. The carver's mallet has a heavy rounded head that allows a chisel or gouge to be struck from practically any angle. Gripping a gouge or chisel as shown, control the angle and direction of the blade by flexing and rotating your wrist while applying short, sharp blows with the mallet.

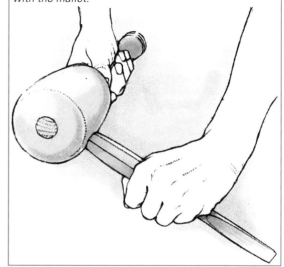

CHIP CARVING

Chip carving is a traditional craft, based on a series of shallow cuts that combine to make regular geometric patterns. You can create a form of chip carving with chisels and gouges, but skilled exponents use knives designed for the purpose.

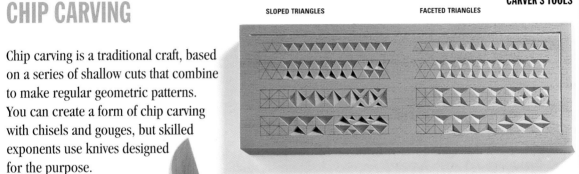

SLOPED TRIANGLES   FACETED TRIANGLES

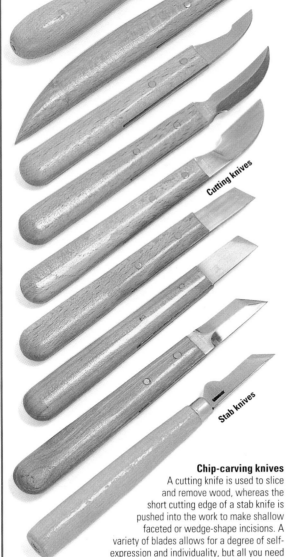

Cutting knives

Stab knives

Chip-carving knives
A cutting knife is used to slice and remove wood, whereas the short cutting edge of a stab knife is pushed into the work to make shallow faceted or wedge-shape incisions. A variety of blades allows for a degree of self-expression and individuality, but all you need for basic chip carving is a straight cutting knife.

Cutting sloped triangles

Mark out the pattern in pencil. Place the point of a cutting knife on the apex of a triangle and press straight down into the wood to a depth of about ⅛in (3mm). Keeping the blade upright, draw the knife towards you until the point rises out to the surface at the base line. Repeat the cut on the other side; then, with the blade held at a shallow angle, slice along the base line to remove the chip of wood.

Cutting faceted triangles

To cut one side of a faceted triangle, place the point of the knife on one corner and hold the blade at an angle to the surface. Draw the blade towards you, pressing down into the wood, then pull out to the surface again as you reach the opposite corner of the triangle. Repeat the cut on all three sides, ensuring that they meet at a point in the center of the triangle.

Depending on grain direction, it may be more convenient to make some cuts with a push stroke.

Examples of basic chip carving

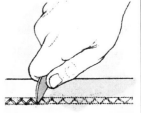

1 Cut from the apex towards the base line

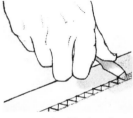

2 Slice out the chip of wood

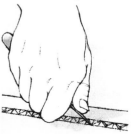

1 Cut towards you, pressing down then out to the corner

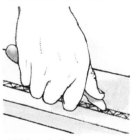

2 Make a similar cut with a push stroke

125

SHARPENING CARVING TOOLS

New carving tools are ground with beveled cutting edges that require honing on a whetstone (see pages 94–5) before they are ready for use. Honing a carving chisel or gouge not only produces a razor-sharp edge, it also rounds off the heel of each bevel so that the tool can cut into the wood from practically any angle. You will need to resharpen your tools at frequent intervals.

Sharpening a carving chisel
Start with the ground bevel held flat on the whetstone. Draw the chisel backwards while lowering the handle, then push forward and raise the handle to rub the cutting edge along the stone. Repeat this action again and again until you have honed a sharp edge and rounded the heel on both sides of the blade. Polish the edge with a strop.

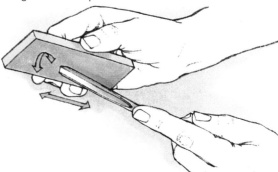

Sharpening a gouge
Hold a gouge at right angles to the stone, with the ground bevel resting on the surface. Rub the tool back and forth along the stone, simultaneously rolling the blade from side to side. Introducing a rocking motion, by alternately raising and lowering the handle, will round over the bevel at the same time.

Sharpening a parting tool
Hone the two sides of a V-shape parting tool like a pair of chisels; then carefully radius the point where they meet, using a slipstone. Work the inner bevel with a knife-edge slip (see pages 94–5).

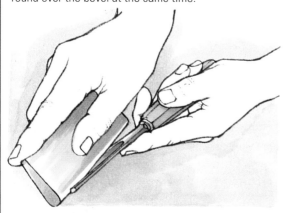

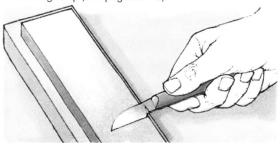

Removing the burr
Honing the convex edge of a gouge raises a burr on the inside which must be removed using a slipstone or cone (see pages 94–5). Work the stone back and forth with a rocking motion to shape a rounded shoulder behind the cutting edge. Finish by stropping the edge on a strip of leather or with a powered wheel (see page 98).

Sharpening chip-carving knives
Place a straight chip-carving knife on a whetstone, with the cutting edge held at a shallow angle to the surface. Rub the blade back and forth along the stone, keeping the entire cutting edge in contact with the surface. Turn the knife over and hone the other side. Sharpen a stab knife in a similar way, but hold the cutting edge at about 30 degrees to the stone. Finally, strop each tool to a razor-sharp cutting edge.